CHICKEN BREAST ENHANCEMENTS

Printed in the United States of America
by G&R Publishing Co.

Distributed By:

507 Industrial Street
Waverly, IA 50677

ISBN-13: 978-1-56383-436-3
ISBN-10: 1-56383-436-7
Item #7076

What's Inside

DISCLAIMER
NO STEROIDS WERE USED IN THE CREATION OF THIS CONTENT.

Your Guide to the Best Breasts

Bring home the best breasts

At the store, packages of chicken should feel cold to the touch and should be among the last items you select before checking out.

Packages of chicken should be wrapped in plastic bags to prevent leaking onto other items in your grocery cart.

Breasts come in three basic forms: bone-in, skin-on (which is typically the cheapest); boneless, skin-on; and boneless, skinless (which is typically the most expensive) and two basic sizes: whole and half.

Take care when handling breasts

Store fresh chicken breasts in a refrigerator that maintains a temperature of 40°F or colder, and use them within 2 days. Otherwise, they should be frozen.

Never thaw frozen breasts at room temperature. Plan ahead. It could take a couple of days for them to fully thaw.

Wash hands and cutting boards thoroughly after handling fresh raw breasts and never place cooked breast meat or other food on the same surface previously used to hold raw breast meat without first washing the surface with soap and hot water.

After marinating chicken breasts, discard marinade. If you wish to brush marinade over chicken while cooking, reserve a portion of the marinade before adding chicken.

After cooking, serve breasts hot; otherwise, chill promptly. Chill any leftovers as soon as the meal is over.

Prep breasts for a meal

Marinades add flavor, moisture and tenderness to breast meat. To make quick work of marinating chicken breasts with no clean-up, place marinade and breasts together in a zippered plastic bag. Seal the bag and turn several times until breast meat is well coated. Alternately, place breasts in a bowl and pour marinade over the top. Turn breasts several times until well coated.

Dry rubs are a combination of spices and seasonings without wet ingredients. Rubs increase breast meat's natural browning and help give the meat wonderful flavor. Simply sprinkle rub mixture over the breast meat and gently pat or massage it in with your fingers.

Breast meat can be cut into pieces before or after it has been cooked. If cutting before cooking, cut pieces of similar size to ensure even cooking. You may find it easiest to cut uncooked meat with kitchen shears.

To flatten chicken breasts, place one breast at a time between two pieces of plastic wrap and pound with the flat side of a meat mallet.

Cook breasts to an internal temperature of 165° to 170° or until juices run clear when cut with a knife at the thickest part and chicken is no longer pink inside.

SOAKS, RUBS & BODY BUTTERS

Be sure to discard any unused rub or marinade mixture that comes in contact with raw chicken.

Breast Enhancement Tip #1

Breasts will be perkier after a good long soak or a gentle rub. Try these recipes for rubs, marinades and butters and see for yourself.

Sweet & Spicy Rub

Coats about 3 lbs. chicken

Ingredients

2 T. brown sugar

1 tsp. paprika

½ tsp. chili powder

½ tsp. cayenne pepper

1 tsp. black pepper

½ tsp. ground cumin

½ tsp. garlic powder

1 tsp. dried oregano

Directions

In a small bowl, stir together brown sugar, paprika, chili powder, cayenne pepper, black pepper, cumin, garlic powder and oregano.

Cooking Idea: *Coat all sides of bone-in chicken breasts with Sweet & Spicy Rub and place in a baking pan. Bake in a 350° oven for 45 to 50 minutes or until juices run clear.*

Big Batch Cumin-Fennel Rub

*Coats about 8 lbs. chicken**

Ingredients

2 T. salt

¼ C. sugar

2 T. ground cumin

1 tsp. black pepper

½ tsp. cayenne pepper

2 T. ground fennel

¼ C. paprika

Directions

In a small bowl, stir together salt, sugar, cumin, black pepper, cayenne pepper, fennel and paprika.

Cooking Idea: *Coat all sides of boneless, skinless chicken breast halves with Big Batch Cumin-Fennel Rub and set aside about 15 minutes. Grill over medium heat for 12 to 15 minutes or until cooked through, turning occasionally. Cover with aluminum foil and set aside for 15 minutes before serving.*

* Store extra Big Batch Cumin-Fennel Rub in an airtight container to have on hand for future meals.

Big Batch Pantry Rub

Coats about 18 lbs. chicken*

Ingredients

½ C. paprika

3 T. cayenne pepper

5 T. black pepper

⅓ C. garlic powder

3 T. onion powder

6 T. salt

2½ T. dried oregano

2½ T. dried thyme

Directions

In a medium bowl, stir together paprika, cayenne pepper, black pepper, garlic powder, onion powder, salt, oregano and thyme.

Cooking Idea: *Coat all sides of boneless, skinless chicken breast halves with desired amount of Big Batch Pantry Rub and place in a baking pan. Bake in a 350° oven for 35 to 40 minutes or until juices run clear.*

* Store extra Big Batch Pantry Rub in an airtight container to have on hand for future meals.

Chili-Spice Blend

Coats about 3 lbs. chicken

Ingredients

2 T. brown sugar

1 T. chili powder

1 T. paprika

1½ tsp. ground cumin

¼ tsp. cayenne pepper

1½ tsp. garlic powder

1½ tsp. dry mustard

1 tsp. salt

1 tsp. black pepper

Directions

In a medium bowl, stir together brown sugar, chili powder, paprika, cumin, cayenne pepper, garlic powder, dry mustard, salt and black pepper.

Cooking Idea: *Coat all sides of boneless, skinless chicken breast halves with Chili-Spice Blend and refrigerate overnight. Grill over medium heat for 12 to 15 minutes or until juices run clear, turning occasionally.*

Chili-Lime Sublime

Coats about 2 lbs. chicken

Ingredients

4 tsp. chili powder

4 tsp. brown sugar

4 tsp. lime zest

1 tsp. salt

½ tsp. garlic powder

¼ tsp. cayenne pepper

Directions

In a small bowl, mix together chili powder, brown sugar, lime zest, salt, garlic powder and cayenne pepper.

Cooking Idea: *Coat all sides of boneless, skinless chicken breast halves with Chili-Lime Sublime and refrigerate for 30 minutes. Grill over medium heat for 12 to 15 minutes or until juices run clear, turning once or twice.*

Clove-Spice Rub-Down

Coats about 1 lb. chicken

Ingredients

2 tsp. black peppercorns

2 tsp. coriander seed

2 bay leaves

3 whole cloves

1 tsp. Kosher or sea salt

Directions

Grind peppercorns, coriander seed, bay leaves and cloves to desired texture using a mortar and pestle or coffee grinder. Stir in salt.

Cooking Idea: *Coat all sides of bone-in chicken breasts with Clove-Spice Rub-Down and place in a baking pan. Bake in a 350° oven for 45 to 50 minutes or until juices run clear.*

Big Batch Hot & Smoky Dry Rub

Coats about 14 lbs. chicken*

Ingredients

½ C. brown sugar

¼ C. seasoned salt

½ C. smoked paprika

1 T. garlic powder

2 tsp. onion powder

1 T. celery salt

2 T. hot chili powder

2 T. black pepper

1 T. dried sage

1 tsp. ground allspice

1 tsp. ground cumin

¼ to ½ tsp. cayenne pepper

¼ tsp. ground mace

Pinch of ground cloves

Directions

Spread brown sugar on a plate for 1 hour to dry out.

In a food processor, combine brown sugar, seasoned salt, paprika, garlic powder, onion powder, celery salt, chili powder, black pepper, sage, allspice, cumin, cayenne pepper, mace and cloves. Process until well mixed.

Cooking Idea: *Coat all sides of bone-in, skinless chicken breast halves with Big Batch Hot & Smoky Dry Rub; refrigerate for 1 hour. Arrange in a greased slow cooker, bone side down. Cover and cook on low for 5 to 6 hours.*

* Store extra Big Batch Hot & Smoky Dry Rub in an airtight container to have on hand for future meals.

Lemon-Garlic Marinade

Marinates about 4 lbs. chicken

Ingredients

⅔ C. lemon juice
⅓ C. dry white wine
3 T. olive oil

¼ C. chopped fresh parsley
1 bulb garlic, cloves separated, peeled and chopped

Directions

In a large bowl, whisk together lemon juice, wine, olive oil, parsley and garlic.

Cooking Idea: *Season bone-in chicken breast halves with salt and black pepper and place in a baking pan. Pour Lemon-Garlic Marinade over chicken; cover and refrigerate for 20 to 30 minutes. Discard marinade and bake chicken in a 375° oven for 40 to 45 minutes or until juices run clear.*

Herb-licious Marinade

Marinates about 2 lbs. chicken

Ingredients

2 T. balsamic or red wine vinegar

1 T. dried crushed herbs*

1 T. whole grain or Dijon mustard

1 tsp. garlic powder

1 tsp. onion powder

¼ C. olive oil

Directions

In a small bowl, whisk together vinegar, herbs, mustard, garlic powder, onion powder and olive oil.

Cooking Idea: *Transfer Herb-licious Marinade to a large zippered plastic bag. Close bag and turn to mix. Add bone-in chicken breast halves. Close bag and turn to coat chicken. Refrigerate for 30 minutes. Discard marinade and bake chicken in a 375° oven for 40 to 45 minutes or until juices run clear.*

* Try thyme, oregano and/or rosemary.

Teriyaki Marinade

Marinates about 3 lbs. chicken

Ingredients

¼ C. brown sugar

¼ C. vegetable oil

¼ C. soy sauce

¼ C. dry sherry

1 tsp. dry mustard

1 tsp. ground ginger

1 tsp. minced garlic

2 T. molasses

Directions

In a medium bowl, whisk together brown sugar, vegetable oil, soy sauce, sherry, dry mustard, ginger, garlic and molasses.

Cooking Idea: *Place bone-in chicken breast halves in a baking pan. Pour Teriyaki Marinade over chicken; cover and refrigerate overnight. Discard marinade and bake chicken in a 375° oven for 40 to 45 minutes or until juices run clear.*

Honey & Soy Soak

Marinates about 1 1/2 lbs. chicken

Ingredients

¼ C. honey

¼ C. soy sauce

½ tsp. minced garlic

2 T. rice wine vinegar

½ tsp. five spice powder

Directions

In a small bowl, combine honey, soy sauce, garlic, vinegar and five spice powder.

Cooking Idea: *Slice boneless, skinless chicken breast halves into strips and place in a large zippered plastic bag with Honey & Soy Soak. Close bag and turn to coat chicken. Refrigerate overnight. Discard marinade and thread chicken strips onto skewers. Grill over medium heat for 10 to 15 minutes or until cooked through, turning occasionally.*

Citrus Marinade

Marinates about 2¹/₂ lbs. chicken

Ingredients

¼ C. apple cider vinegar
3 T. whole grain mustard
1½ tsp. minced garlic
Juice of 1 lime

Juice of 1 lemon
½ C. brown sugar
1½ tsp. salt
⅓ C. olive oil

Directions

In a large bowl, stir together vinegar, mustard, garlic, lime juice, lemon juice, brown sugar, salt and olive oil.

Cooking Idea: *Place boneless, skinless chicken breast halves in a baking pan. Pour Citrus Marinade over chicken; cover and refrigerate overnight. Discard marinade and grill chicken over medium-low heat for 12 to 15 minutes or until juices run clear, turning occasionally.*

Sweet Italiano

Marinates about 3 lbs. chicken

Ingredients

1 (16 oz.) bottle prepared
Italian salad dressing

⅓ C. lemon juice

⅓ C. honey

¼ C. Worcestershire sauce

2 tsp. paprika

Directions

In a large bowl, stir together salad dressing, lemon juice, honey,
Worcestershire sauce and paprika.

Cooking Idea: *Place boneless, skinless chicken breast halves
in a baking pan. Pour Sweet Italiano over chicken; cover and
refrigerate at least 6 hours. Discard marinade and grill chicken over
medium heat for 12 to 15 minutes or until cooked through, turning
occasionally. Cover with aluminum foil and set aside for 15 minutes
before serving.*

Honey-Lime Immersion

Marinates about 2¹/₂ lbs. chicken

Ingredients

¾ C. honey

⅔ C. lime juice

⅓ C. vegetable oil

1 T. grated fresh gingerroot

2 tsp. minced garlic

Directions

In a small bowl, stir together honey, lime juice, vegetable oil, gingerroot and garlic.

Cooking Idea: *Transfer Honey-Lime Immersion to a large zippered plastic bag. Close bag and turn to mix. Cut boneless, skinless chicken breasts into 1˝ cubes. Add chicken cubes to bag. Close bag and turn to coat chicken. Refrigerate for 1 hour, turning once. Discard marinade, thread chicken cubes onto skewers and grill over medium heat for 12 to 15 minutes or until cooked through, turning once.*

Double Lemon Marinade

Marinates about 1½ lbs. chicken

Ingredients

½ C. chicken broth
1 T. lemon zest
¼ C. lemon juice

¼ tsp. black pepper
1 T. finely chopped fresh
   lemon thyme

Directions

In a small bowl, stir together broth, lemon zest, lemon juice, black pepper and thyme.

Cooking Idea: *Transfer Double Lemon Marinade to a large zippered plastic bag. Close bag and turn to mix. Add boneless, skinless chicken breast halves to bag. Close bag and turn to coat chicken. Refrigerate for 1 to 2 hours, turning occasionally. Discard marinade and grill chicken over medium heat for 12 to 15 minutes or until cooked through. Cut two lemons in half and add to grill, cut sides down, the last three minutes of grilling time. Serve chicken with grilled lemon halves.*

Cilantro Butter

Ingredients

½ C. butter, softened

2 T. finely chopped
  fresh cilantro

1 tsp. minced garlic

2 T. finely chopped onion

½ tsp. salt

¼ tsp. black pepper

Pinch of white pepper

Dash of Worcestershire sauce

Juice of 1 lime

Directions

In a small bowl, stir together butter, cilantro, garlic, onion, salt, black pepper, white pepper, Worcestershire sauce and lime juice until thoroughly combined.

Cooking Idea: *Prepare chicken as desired. Remove from heat and top with Cilantro Butter to taste. Serve immediately. Or add desired amount of Cilantro Butter to hot chicken soup.*

Scampi Butter

Makes about 3/4 cup

Ingredients

½ C. butter, softened
1 T. chopped fresh parsley
1 T. minced garlic
2 T. finely chopped onion
½ tsp. garlic powder
½ tsp. sea salt

¼ tsp. freshly ground
  black pepper
Pinch of white pepper
Dash of Worcestershire sauce
Juice of 1 lemon

Directions

In a small bowl, stir together butter, parsley, garlic, onion, garlic powder, salt, black pepper, white pepper, Worcestershire sauce and lemon juice until thoroughly combined.

Cooking Idea: *Prepare chicken as desired. Remove from heat and top with Scampi Butter to taste. Serve immediately. Or add desired amount of Scampi Butter to hot chicken soup.*

Herb Butter

Makes about 1 cup

Ingredients

1 C. butter, softened

¼ C. chopped fresh herbs*

½ tsp. minced garlic

¼ tsp. salt

Directions

In a small bowl, stir together butter, herbs, garlic and salt until well blended. Roll into a log, wrap in plastic wrap and chill; then cut into slices as desired.

Cooking Idea: *Prepare chicken as desired. Remove from heat and top with a slice of Herb Butter. Serve immediately. Or add desired amount of Herb Butter to hot chicken soup.*

* Try basil, dill, parsley, rosemary, sage and/or tarragon.

Sun-Dried Tomato Butter

Makes about ³/4 cup

Ingredients

½ C. butter, softened
3 T. sun-dried tomatoes,
   finely chopped

1 tsp. minced garlic
1½ T. chopped fresh basil
¼ tsp. salt

Directions

In a small bowl, combine butter, tomatoes, garlic, basil and salt; stir until well blended. Roll into a log, wrap in plastic wrap and chill; then cut into slices as desired.

Cooking Idea: *Prepare chicken as desired. Remove from heat and top with a slice of Sun-Dried Tomato Butter. Serve immediately. Or add desired amount of Sun-Dried Tomato Butter to hot chicken soup.*

IMPLANTS

Choose breasts for stuffing that are fairly thick so a "pocket" can be cut into the thickest part and stuffed with delicious goodness.

Breast Enhancement Tip #2

As with all things, moderation is best. Overstuffing breasts can cause them to pop open, resulting in embarrassing "wardrobe malfunctions." This chapter is stuffed with great recipes.

Basil & Cheese Stuffed Breasts

Serves 4

Ingredients

1 C. shredded
  mozzarella cheese

¼ C. finely chopped
  fresh basil, divided

2 T. heavy cream

1 T. lemon juice

1½ tsp. minced garlic, divided

Salt and black pepper to taste

4 boneless, skinless
  chicken breast halves

¼ C. mayonnaise

1 C. fresh bread crumbs

2 T. olive oil, divided

1 pt. cherry tomatoes, halved

Directions

Preheat oven to 425°. Coat a 9 x 13″ baking pan with nonstick cooking spray; set aside. In a medium bowl, stir together mozzarella cheese, 2 tablespoons basil, cream, lemon juice, 1 teaspoon garlic, salt and black pepper.

Cut a pocket in each chicken breast and stuff with cheese mixture; seal pocket closed using toothpicks. Arrange in prepared baking pan and spread 1 tablespoon mayonnaise evenly over each breast.

In a small bowl, stir together bread crumbs, remaining 2 tablespoons basil, remaining ½ teaspoon garlic and 1 tablespoon olive oil. Sprinkle evenly over chicken, pressing lightly to adhere.

In same small bowl, toss tomatoes with remaining 1 tablespoon olive oil and additional salt and black pepper; arrange around chicken in prepared baking pan. Bake for 25 to 30 minutes or until chicken is cooked through.

Slow-Cooked Bacon-'Shroom Chicken

Serves 6

Ingredients

6 boneless, skinless chicken breast halves

4 bacon strips, cooked until crisp, crumbled

1 (4.5 oz.) jar sliced mushrooms, drained and chopped

2 T. finely chopped fresh sage, divided

1 T. butter, melted

Salt and black pepper to taste

½ C. chicken broth

2 T. flour

2 T. heavy cream

⅓ C. shredded Parmesan cheese

Directions

Spray a 5-quart slow cooker with nonstick cooking spray; set aside. With a meat mallet, pound chicken to ¼″ thickness. In a small bowl, stir together bacon, mushrooms and 1 tablespoon sage; divide mixture evenly among breasts. Roll up breasts, tucking ends under to hold filling. Transfer to slow cooker, seam side down. Brush with butter and season with salt and black pepper. Pour broth around chicken. Cover and cook on low for 3 to 3½ hours.

Transfer chicken to a serving platter; cover with aluminum foil to keep warm. Strain cooking liquid into a medium saucepan, discarding solids. Bring to a boil and whisk in flour; boil for 1 minute or until thickened, stirring constantly. Remove from heat. Stir in cream and remaining 1 tablespoon sage. Pour sauce over chicken and sprinkle with Parmesan cheese.

Smoky Apple & Brie Stuffed Chicken

Serves 4

Ingredients

⅓ C. ketchup
¼ C. apple cider vinegar
2 T. molasses
2 tsp. Worcestershire sauce
Liquid smoke to taste
2 T. butter

1 T. olive oil
½ C. chopped onion
1 green apple, cored
 and chopped
4 oz. Brie cheese, chopped
4 boneless, skin-on
 chicken breast halves

Directions

Preheat oven to 400°. Coat a 9 x 13˝ baking pan with nonstick cooking spray; set aside. In a small bowl, stir together ketchup, vinegar, molasses, Worcestershire sauce and liquid smoke; set aside.

In a large skillet, heat butter and olive oil together over medium heat until butter melts. Add onion and cook for 10 minutes or until tender. Add apple and ¼ cup ketchup mixture to onion mixture. Cook for 5 minutes or until apple is tender, stirring occasionally. Remove from heat and cool slightly; then stir in Brie cheese. Carefully loosen (but do not remove) skin from chicken breasts. Divide onion mixture evenly under skin of each breast and transfer to prepared baking pan, skin side up. Brush 1 tablespoon ketchup mixture over each breast. Bake for 35 to 45 minutes or until cooked through. Remove chicken from pan and keep warm.

Skim fat from pan and transfer drippings to a small saucepan. Add remaining ketchup mixture to saucepan, cooking over medium heat until warm. Remove from heat and pour over chicken.

Simple Stuffed Breasts

Serves 2

Ingredients

1 T. vegetable oil

½ onion, finely chopped

1 celery rib, chopped

1 tsp. hot sauce

1 T. Dijon mustard

2 boneless, skinless
   chicken breast halves

Directions

Heat vegetable oil in a large skillet over medium heat. Add onion and celery; cook until tender. Stir in hot sauce and mustard. Remove from heat.

Preheat grill to medium-high heat. Cut a pocket in each chicken breast half and stuff each with some of the onion mixture. Transfer chicken to skillet and cook over medium heat for 2 to 3 minutes on each side or until lightly browned. Remove from skillet and grill for 10 to 15 minutes on each side or until cooked through. Transfer to a serving platter and pour any remaining onion mixture over the top.

Bacon-Feta Chicken Breasts

Serves 4

Ingredients

4 boneless, skinless
  chicken breast halves

¼ C. crumbled cooked bacon

¼ C. crumbled feta cheese

Salt and black pepper to taste

1 T. canola oil

2 (14.5 oz.) cans diced
  tomatoes, undrained

1 T. dried basil

Directions

Cut a pocket in each chicken breast half and stuff with equal amounts of bacon and feta cheese. Seal pocket closed using toothpicks. Season with salt and black pepper. Heat canola oil in a large skillet over medium heat. Add chicken and cook for 2 to 3 minutes on each side until lightly browned.

Drain one can tomatoes; add to skillet. Reduce heat to low. Stir in remaining tomatoes with juice and sprinkle with basil. Cover and simmer for 10 minutes. Uncover and simmer 5 minutes more or until chicken is cooked through.

Quick Jalapeño-Jack Stuffed Breasts

Serves 2

Ingredients

2 boneless, skinless
chicken breast halves

1 tsp. seasoned salt

Black pepper to taste

2 thin slices Monterey Jack
cheese with jalapeño
peppers

2 red bell pepper rings

Directions

Preheat oven to 350°. With a meat mallet, pound chicken to
¼˝ thickness. Spray both sides of breasts with nonstick cooking
spray and sprinkle with seasoned salt and black pepper. Place one
slice Monterey Jack cheese on each breast half. Roll up breasts
and seal closed using toothpicks. Transfer to an 8 x 8˝ baking
pan, seam side down. Place pepper rings on top and spray with
cooking spray. Bake for 25 to 30 minutes or until cooked through.

Spinach & Crimini Skillet Chicken

Serves 4

Ingredients

4 boneless, skinless
  chicken breast halves
¼ C. butter, divided
12 crimini mushroom caps
1 shallot, quartered
Salt and black pepper to taste
1 (10 oz.) pkg. frozen
  chopped spinach,
  thawed and drained*

1 C. ricotta cheese
½ C. grated Parmesan cheese
½ tsp. ground nutmeg
3 T. olive oil
2 T. flour
½ C. dry white wine
1 C. chicken broth

Directions

With a meat mallet, pound chicken to ¼˝ thickness; set aside. In a medium skillet, melt 2 tablespoons butter over medium heat. Add mushrooms, shallot, salt and black pepper and cook for 5 minutes. Transfer to a food processor and pulse until mushrooms are finely chopped; transfer to a medium bowl. Stir in spinach, ricotta and Parmesan cheeses and nutmeg. Divide mushroom mixture among breast halves; roll up and seal closed using toothpicks. Return skillet to stove and heat olive oil over medium-high heat. Add stuffed breasts and cook for 10 to 12 minutes or until brown on all sides. Remove from pan.

In same skillet over medium-high heat, melt remaining 2 tablespoons butter. Whisk in flour and cook for 1 minute. Whisk in wine and cook 1 minute longer. Whisk in broth and return breasts to skillet. Reduce heat to low and simmer until chicken is cooked through and sauce is warm. Transfer chicken to a serving platter and pour sauce over the top.

* Place thawed spinach on a clean kitchen towel. Above the sink, squeeze towel around spinach to remove all excess liquid.

Loaded & Tied Chicken

Serves 4

Ingredients

3 T. olive oil, divided
¼ C. raisins
¼ C. pine nuts
1 T. minced garlic
1 lb. fresh spinach, trimmed
Salt and black pepper to taste

¼ C. panko bread crumbs
4 boneless, skinless
   chicken breast halves
2 T. balsamic vinegar
1 T. Dijon mustard

Directions

Preheat oven to 350°. In a large oven-safe skillet over medium-high heat, heat 2 tablespoons olive oil. Add raisins, pine nuts and garlic. Cook for 30 seconds, stirring constantly; add spinach. Season with salt and black pepper. Cook for 10 minutes or until spinach is wilted, stirring constantly. Remove from skillet and coarsely chop. Stir in bread crumbs.

With a meat mallet, flatten chicken breasts slightly. With flattest side of breasts facing up, cover two breast halves with spinach mixture. Position remaining two breast halves on top, facing the opposite direction so the tapered end of one breast half sets on top of the rounded end of the other. Roll up each pair of breasts together and tie in three places with kitchen string. Sprinkle all sides with additional salt and black pepper. Add remaining 1 tablespoon olive oil to pan and roll chicken in oil to coat. Arrange chicken in skillet and set in oven. Bake for 30 to 40 minutes until cooked through, turning once during cooking. Transfer chicken to a serving platter and tent loosely with aluminum foil.

Place skillet on stove and add vinegar, mustard and ¼ cup water. Cook over medium heat until sauce thickens slightly, stirring often. Remove strings from chicken and slice breasts crosswise into pieces. Drizzle with sauce.

Apple-Stuffed Chicken

Serves 4

Ingredients

- 2 boneless, skinless chicken breasts
- ½ C. chopped apple, any variety
- 2 T. shredded Cheddar cheese
- 1 T. Italian seasoned dry bread crumbs
- 1 T. butter
- ¼ C. dry white wine
- 1½ tsp. cornstarch
- 1 T. chopped fresh parsley

Directions

With a meat mallet, pound chicken to ¼˝ thickness. In a small bowl, stir together apple, Cheddar cheese and bread crumbs. Divide apple mixture evenly among chicken breasts; roll up breasts and seal closed using toothpicks.

In a medium skillet over medium heat, melt butter. Add chicken and brown on all sides. Add wine and ¼ cup water. Reduce heat to low, cover and simmer for 15 to 20 minutes or until chicken is cooked through. Transfer chicken to a serving platter and tent with aluminum foil.

In a small bowl, stir together cornstarch and 1 tablespoon water until smooth. Add cornstarch mixture to juices in pan and cook over medium heat until thickened, whisking constantly; pour over chicken. Slice chicken as desired and garnish with parsley.

Broccoli Stuffers

Serves 4

Ingredients

4 boneless, skinless
chicken breast halves

1 egg

4 tsp. butter, melted
and cooled

¾ C. seasoned dry bread
crumbs, any variety

1 T. Parmesan cheese

Salt and black pepper to taste

¼ C. shredded
mozzarella cheese

2 oz. sliced deli ham

½ C. chopped cooked broccoli

Directions

Preheat oven to 375°. Coat a 9 x 13″ baking pan with nonstick
cooking spray; set aside. With a meat mallet, pound chicken to
¼″ thickness. In a small bowl, whisk together egg and butter.
On a plate, stir together bread crumbs, Parmesan cheese, salt
and black pepper. Dip both sides of each breast half in egg
mixture, then in crumb mixture, turning to coat evenly. Divide
mozzarella cheese, ham and broccoli evenly on top of each
breast half. Roll up and seal closed using toothpicks. Transfer to
prepared baking pan, seam side down. Bake for 40 minutes or
until cooked through.

Stuffing Stuffers

Serves 6

Ingredients

¼ C. butter, cubed

1 (6 oz.) pkg. chicken-flavored stuffing mix

1 egg, beaten

6 boneless, skinless chicken breast halves

¼ C. butter, melted

Salt and black pepper to taste

1 (10.7 oz.) can cream of mushroom soup

¼ tsp. dried dill weed

Directions

Preheat oven to 400°. Coat a 9 x 13˝ baking pan with nonstick cooking spray; set aside. In a medium bowl, combine butter and 1½ cups hot water, stirring until butter is melted. Stir in stuffing mix and egg.

With a meat mallet, pound chicken to ¼˝ thickness. Divide stuffing mixture evenly among breast halves. Roll up breasts, tucking ends under to hold filling; transfer to prepared baking pan, seam side down. Brush with melted butter and season with salt and black pepper. Bake for 35 minutes or until cooked through.

In a small saucepan over medium heat, stir together soup, dill weed and ½ cup water until hot. Pour over chicken.

Ranch & Rice Stuffed Breasts

Serves 8

Ingredients

2 T. cream cheese, softened
1 C. shredded Cheddar cheese
1 C. cooked white rice
1 C. frozen chopped broccoli, thawed and drained

8 boneless, skinless chicken breast halves
¼ C. ranch salad dressing

Directions

Preheat oven to 350°. Coat a 9 x 13˝ baking pan with nonstick cooking spray; set aside. In a medium bowl, stir together cream cheese, Cheddar cheese, rice and broccoli; set aside.

With a meat mallet, pound chicken to ¼˝ thickness. Top each with an equal amount of rice mixture. Roll up breasts, tucking ends under to hold filling. Transfer to prepared baking pan, seam side down. Drizzle salad dressing evenly over chicken. Bake for 35 to 40 minutes or until cooked through.

Bacon-Cheddar Stuffed Chicken

Serves 4

Ingredients

4 boneless, skinless chicken breast halves

4 bacon strips, cooked until crisp, crumbled

2 oz. sharp Cheddar cheese, cubed

½ tsp. salt

¼ tsp. black pepper

¼ tsp. paprika

1 T. olive oil

1 tsp. cornstarch

⅔ C. chicken broth

2 T. chopped fresh parsley

Directions

Cut a pocket in each chicken breast half and stuff with equal amounts of bacon and Cheddar cheese; seal pocket closed using toothpicks. Season with salt, black pepper and paprika.

In a large skillet over medium-high heat, heat olive oil. Add chicken breasts and cook for 8 minutes or until browned, turning once during cooking time. Reduce heat to medium-low, cover and cook 10 minutes more or until chicken is cooked through. Remove chicken from skillet and tent loosely with aluminum foil.

In a small bowl, stir together cornstarch and broth until smooth. Add mixture to skillet and bring to a boil over medium heat, scraping up browned bits from bottom of skillet. Cook for 3 minutes or until thickened. Add parsley and pour over chicken.

Mexican-Style Chicken

Serves 4

Ingredients

½ C. butter, melted
½ C. dry bread crumbs
¼ C. grated Parmesan cheese
½ tsp. dried cumin
1 tsp. chili powder
Salt and black pepper to taste

4 boneless, skinless
chicken breast halves

1 C. shredded Mexican
cheese blend

½ C. pickled jalapeño peppers,
drained and chopped

Directions

Preheat oven to 350°. Coat a 9 x 13˝ baking pan with nonstick cooking spray. Pour butter on a large plate. In a large zippered plastic bag, combine bread crumbs, Parmesan cheese, cumin, chili powder, salt and black pepper; close bag and shake to blend.

With a meat mallet, pound chicken to ¼˝ thickness. Dip chicken in melted butter and transfer to plastic bag. Close bag and shake to coat chicken evenly with crumb mixture. Top each breast half with an equal amount of Mexican cheese blend and jalapeño peppers. Roll up breasts and seal closed using toothpicks. Transfer to prepared baking pan, seam side down. Bake for 40 minutes or until chicken is cooked through.

Italian Breasts

Serves 4

Ingredients

4 boneless, skinless chicken breast halves, butterflied*

1 tsp. dried Italian seasoning

2 T. grated Parmesan cheese

¼ C. chopped fresh chives

½ (12 oz.) jar roasted red peppers, drained

¼ C. shredded mozzarella cheese

Salt and black pepper to taste

2 T. olive oil

Directions

Preheat oven to 350°. Coat a 9 x 13˝ baking pan with nonstick cooking spray; set aside. With a meat mallet, pound chicken to ¼˝ thickness. In a small bowl, stir together Italian seasoning, Parmesan cheese and chives; sprinkle mixture evenly over chicken. Place three red pepper strips on each butterflied breast. Top each with an equal amount of mozzarella cheese. Roll up and seal closed using toothpicks. Transfer to prepared baking pan, seam side down. Season with salt and black pepper and drizzle with olive oil. Bake for 15 minutes. Set oven to broil and continue baking for 5 to 10 minutes or until cooked through.

To butterfly, place a chicken breast half on a flat work surface. Starting at the thickest side of breast, hold a sharp knife parallel to work surface and slice almost completely through chicken until you are able to open breast like a book.

Wine-y Onion-Stuffed Chicken

Serves 4

Ingredients

2 T. olive oil, divided

1½ C. thinly sliced red onion

2 tsp. chopped fresh rosemary, divided

Salt and black pepper to taste

⅔ C. shredded fontina, Gouda or Monterey Jack cheese

4 boneless, skinless chicken breast halves

½ C. dry white wine

1 C. chicken broth

1½ T. flour

Directions

Heat 1 tablespoon olive oil in a large skillet over medium-high heat. Add onion and 1 teaspoon rosemary. Cook for 6 to 7 minutes or until onion is golden brown, stirring occasionally. Season with salt and black pepper. Remove from heat and let cool. Then stir in fontina cheese. Cut a pocket in each chicken breast half and stuff with an equal amount of cheese mixture; seal pocket closed using toothpicks.

In the same skillet over medium-high heat, heat remaining 1 tablespoon olive oil. Add chicken and cook for 10 minutes or until golden brown on both sides, turning halfway through cooking. Transfer chicken to a plate and cover with aluminum foil.

Add wine and remaining 1 teaspoon rosemary to same skillet. Cook over medium-high heat for 2 minutes. In a small bowl, whisk together broth and flour until smooth; add to skillet, reduce heat to low and whisk for 1 minute or until sauce thickens. Return chicken to skillet and spoon some of the sauce over the top. Cover and cook for 3 to 4 minutes or until chicken is just cooked through. Serve sauce with chicken.

Bruschetta Breasts with Onion Vinaigrette

Serves 8

Ingredients

- 1 (14.5 oz.) can diced Italian herb tomatoes, undrained
- ¼ C. chopped fresh basil
- 1¼ C. shredded mozzarella cheese, divided
- 1 (6 oz.) pkg. chicken-flavored stuffing mix
- 8 boneless, skinless chicken breast halves
- ⅓ C. Vidalia onion with roasted red pepper vinaigrette

Directions

Preheat oven to 350°. Coat a 9 x 13″ baking pan with nonstick cooking spray; set aside. In a large bowl, combine tomatoes with juice, basil and ½ cup mozzarella cheese. Add stuffing mix; stir until just moistened. With a meat mallet, pound chicken to ¼″ thickness. Divide stuffing mixture evenly among breast halves. Roll up breasts, tucking ends under to hold filling; transfer to prepared baking pan, seam side down. Drizzle with vinaigrette. Bake for 40 minutes or until chicken is cooked through. Top with remaining ¾ cup mozzarella cheese, and bake 5 minutes more or until cheese is melted.

Stuffed Santa Fe Chicken

Serves 8

Ingredients

¾ C. butter, divided

1 C. Italian seasoned dry bread crumbs

1½ T. grated Parmesan cheese

½ tsp. salt

½ tsp. black pepper

½ tsp. ground cumin

8 boneless, skinless chicken breast halves

12 thin slices Monterey Jack cheese

5 to 6 T. flour

1 C. milk

1 red bell pepper, diced

1 green bell pepper, diced

Directions

Coat a 9 x 13″ baking pan with nonstick cooking spray; set aside. In a microwave-safe pie plate or shallow bowl, melt ½ cup butter. In a separate pie plate, stir together bread crumbs, Parmesan cheese, salt, black pepper and cumin. With a meat mallet, pound chicken to ¼″ thickness. Place one Monterey Jack cheese slice on each breast. Roll up breasts and seal closed using toothpicks. Roll chicken in melted butter and then dredge in bread crumb mixture. Transfer to prepared baking pan, seam side down. Drizzle any remaining butter over chicken. Cover and refrigerate for 1 hour.

Preheat oven to 400°. Uncover chicken and bake for 25 to 30 minutes or until cooked through. Meanwhile, in a small saucepan over medium heat, melt remaining ¼ cup butter. Whisk in flour until smooth. Slowly whisk in milk. Bring mixture to a simmer, stirring constantly. Reduce heat to low, add remaining four cheese slices and stir until cheese melts and mixture is smooth, stirring constantly. Keep warm.

Transfer chicken to individual serving plates and drizzle with cheese mixture. Sprinkle with red and green bell peppers.

Cheesy Asparagus Chicken

Serves 6

Ingredients

6 fresh asparagus spears

1 C. dry bread crumbs

½ C. grated Parmesan cheese

½ C. finely chopped pine nuts

3 eggs

6 boneless, skinless chicken breast halves

Salt and black pepper to taste

3 oz. colby cheese, cut into ½ x 3″ sticks

6 oz. prepared pesto sauce, any variety

1 C. heavy cream

Directions

Preheat oven to 400°. Coat a 9 x 13″ baking pan with nonstick cooking spray; set aside. Snap off tough bottoms from asparagus and discard. Place asparagus in a medium bowl and cover with boiling water. Cover bowl and let set for 1 minute. Drain, rinse with cold water and pat dry. Cut each asparagus spear crosswise into 3″ lengths. In a pie plate or shallow bowl, stir together bread crumbs, Parmesan cheese and pine nuts. In a separate pie plate or shallow bowl, beat eggs.

With a meat mallet, pound chicken to ¼″ thickness and season with salt and black pepper. Place one colby cheese stick and one asparagus piece side by side on each chicken breast; roll up and seal closed using toothpicks. Dip both sides of each chicken breast in egg and then dredge in bread crumb mixture. Dip again in egg and bread crumb mixtures. Transfer to prepared baking pan, seam side down, and bake for 20 to 25 minutes or until cooked through.

Meanwhile, in a small saucepan, stir together pesto sauce and cream. Bring to a boil over medium heat, then cook for 2 minutes until slightly thickened, stirring constantly. Transfer chicken to individual serving plates and pour sauce over the top of each.

SIZE MATTERS

Whole breasts are basically two breast halves still connected in the middle. Chicken breast halves weigh about 4 to 6 ounces; double that for a whole chicken breast. While most of the whole breast recipes in this chapter are written for each to serve two people, adjust the serving size if you want to serve one whole breast per person.

Breast Enhancement Tip #3

Don't kid yourself – size really does matter. However, whether they're a voluptuous full size or a smaller half size, they're fully embraced and loved in this chapter. Try these breast recipes on for size.

Picnic Buttermilk-Pecan Chicken

Serves 3

Ingredients

3 boneless, skinless chicken breast halves

2 C. buttermilk

2 C. pecans

¼ C. panko bread crumbs

5 sprigs fresh parsley

½ tsp. paprika

½ tsp. dry mustard

1 tsp. salt, plus more to taste

Black pepper to taste

2 T. butter

2 T. flour

2 C. milk

2 T. chopped fresh herbs*

Directions

With a meat mallet, pound chicken to ¼˝ thickness. Transfer to a medium bowl. Add buttermilk and turn to coat breasts. Cover and refrigerate for at least 1 hour or up to 8 hours.

Preheat oven to 350°. Line a rimmed baking sheet with parchment paper and set a wire rack on top. Spray rack with nonstick cooking spray; set aside.

In a food processor, combine pecans, bread crumbs, parsley, paprika, dry mustard, 1 teaspoon salt and black pepper. Process until finely ground. Transfer to a plate. Remove chicken from bowl and dredge in pecan mixture. Place on prepared rack. Bake for 20 minutes or until cooked through and crispy.

Meanwhile, in a medium skillet over medium-high heat, melt butter. Add flour and whisk until smooth. Slowly add milk, cooking for 5 minutes or until thickened and smooth, whisking constantly. Stir in herbs. Season with additional salt and black pepper. Pour mixture over chicken.

*Try parsley, thyme, oregano, chives and/or marjoram.

Chicken Parm

Serves 6

Ingredients

½ C. flour

Salt and black pepper to taste

6 boneless, skinless
chicken breast halves

½ C. olive oil

2 T. butter

1 onion, chopped

2 tsp. minced garlic

¾ C. red wine

3 (15 oz.) cans crushed
tomatoes, undrained

2 T. sugar

1 (16 oz.) pkg.
uncooked linguine

1 C. grated Parmesan cheese

Chopped fresh parsley

Directions

Preheat oven to 150°. On a plate, stir together flour, salt and black pepper. With a meat mallet, pound chicken to ¼˝ thickness. Press both sides of chicken into flour mixture. In a large saucepan over medium heat, heat olive oil and butter together until butter is melted. Add chicken and cook for 6 minutes or until golden brown on both sides, turning halfway through cooking time. Transfer breasts to a rimmed baking sheet, cover with aluminum foil and place in oven to keep warm.

Add onion and garlic to oil in skillet and cook for 2 minutes, stirring constantly. Add wine, cooking for 1 to 2 minutes or until reduced by about half, scraping up any browned bits from bottom of saucepan. Add tomatoes with juice and stir to combine. Stir in sugar and additional salt and black pepper. Cook for 30 minutes. Meanwhile, in a large saucepan of boiling water, cook linguine according to package directions; drain.

Arrange chicken breasts on top of sauce in saucepan; cover chicken with Parmesan cheese. Cover skillet, reduce heat to low and simmer until cheese is melted and chicken is cooked through.

Transfer cooked linguine to a serving plate, cover with sauce and arrange breasts on top. Sprinkle with parsley.

Marsala-Baked Chicken

Serves 4

Ingredients

¼ C. dry bread crumbs

¼ C. grated Parmesan cheese

1 T. dried parsley flakes

¼ tsp. paprika

4 boneless, skinless
  chicken breasts halves

Salt and black pepper to taste

2 T. butter

⅓ C. Marsala wine

Directions

Preheat oven to 350°. Coat a 9 x 13″ baking pan with nonstick cooking spray; set aside. In a pie plate, stir together bread crumbs, Parmesan cheese, parsley flakes and paprika. With a meat mallet, pound chicken to ¼″ thickness; season with salt and black pepper. Dredge breasts in bread crumb mixture and arrange in prepared baking pan. Dot each breast with a bit of butter. Cover with aluminum foil and bake for 30 minutes. Pour wine over chicken, cover with foil and bake again for 15 minutes. Uncover and bake 15 minutes longer.

Blue & Bacon Breasts

Serves 4

Ingredients

½ C. plus 4 tsp. butter, softened, divided

2 oz. blue cheese, crumbled

2 bacon strips, cooked until crisp, crumbled

2 tsp. chopped fresh chives

4 bone-in, skin-on chicken breast halves

Black pepper to taste

Directions

Preheat oven to 425°. Coat a 9 x 13″ baking pan with nonstick cooking spray; set aside. In a large bowl, stir together ½ cup butter, blue cheese, bacon and chives. Carefully loosen (but do not remove) skin from chicken breasts. Spread butter mixture evenly under skin of each breast. Spread 1 teaspoon butter over the top of each breast. Transfer breasts to prepared baking pan, skin side up. Season with black pepper. Bake for 35 to 40 minutes or until cooked through. Let stand for 10 minutes before serving.

Corny Baked Chicken

Serves 5

Ingredients

1 C. crushed flaked corn cereal
¼ C. grated Parmesan cheese
Salt and black pepper to taste

5 boneless, skinless
  chicken breast halves
¼ C. mayonnaise

Directions

Preheat oven to 350°. Coat a 9 x 13˝ baking pan with nonstick cooking spray; set aside. In a small bowl, stir together cereal, Parmesan cheese, salt and black pepper. Brush both sides of chicken evenly with mayonnaise, and then press both sides into cereal mixture; arrange in prepared baking pan. Bake for 1 hour or until cooked through.

Quick Swiss Chicken

Serves 6

Ingredients

6 boneless, skinless chicken breast halves

1 (10.7 oz.) can cream of chicken soup

½ C. white wine

6 slices Swiss cheese

1 C. crushed seasoned croutons, any variety

Directions

Preheat oven to 350°. Coat a 9 x 13˝ baking pan with nonstick cooking spray and arrange chicken in pan. In a small bowl, stir together soup and wine and pour over chicken. Top with Swiss cheese slices and sprinkle with crushed croutons. Cover with aluminum foil and bake for 20 minutes. Uncover and bake 15 to 20 minutes more or until cooked through.

Puffed-Up Chicken Wellington

Serves 4

Ingredients

1 puff pastry sheet
   from a 17.3 oz. pkg.

1 egg

2 T. butter, divided

4 boneless, skinless
   chicken breast halves

½ tsp. dried thyme, crushed

Salt and black pepper to taste

¾ C. sliced fresh mushrooms

1 onion, finely chopped

1 T. chopped fresh parsley

1 (3 oz.) pkg. cream cheese,
   softened

1 T. Dijon mustard

Directions

Let pastry sheet set at room temperature for 30 minutes. Preheat oven to 400°. Coat a 9 x 13″ baking pan with nonstick cooking spray. In a small bowl, mix together egg and 1 tablespoon water. Set all aside.

In a large skillet over medium heat, melt 1 tablespoon butter. Add chicken and sprinkle with thyme, salt and black pepper. Cook until browned on both sides. Transfer to a plate, cover and refrigerate for at least 15 minutes.

Meanwhile, melt remaining 1 tablespoon butter in same skillet. Add mushrooms and onion; cook until tender. Stir in parsley. In a small bowl, stir together cream cheese and mustard. On a lightly floured surface, unfold pastry and roll into a 14″ square. Cut into four even squares. Place about 1 tablespoon mushroom mixture in the center of each square. Top each with a chicken breast half. Divide cream cheese mixture among breasts and spread evenly. Brush edges of pastry squares with some of the set-aside egg mixture. Fold all four corners of pastry to the center of chicken, pressing edges together to seal. Transfer to prepared baking pan, seam side down. Brush with more egg mixture. Bake for 25 minutes or until golden brown.

Crispy Seasoned Chicken

Serves 8

Ingredients

1 clove garlic

8 bone-in, skin-on
   chicken breast halves

1 C. fresh parsley, chopped

1½ tsp. salt

½ tsp. black pepper

2 T. olive oil

Directions

Preheat oven to 400°. Set a rimmed baking sheet in the oven to preheat. Cut garlic into eight slices. Carefully loosen (but do not remove) skin from chicken breasts. Place one garlic slice under skin of each breast. Divide parsley evenly among breasts, tucking under skin. Sprinkle each with some of the salt and black pepper.

In a large skillet over medium-high heat, heat 1 tablespoon olive oil. Add half the chicken, skin side down, and cook for 5 minutes or until golden brown. Transfer breasts to preheated baking sheet. Repeat with remaining oil and chicken. Bake for 25 minutes or until skin is crisp and chicken is cooked through. Remove from oven and let set for 5 minutes before serving.

Chinese-Style Apricot-Glazed Chicken

Serves 4

Ingredients

¼ C. chicken broth

2 T. hoisin sauce

1 T. apricot preserves

4 boneless, skinless chicken breast halves

Salt and black pepper to taste

1 T. vegetable oil

Directions

In a small bowl, stir together broth, hoisin sauce and preserves; set aside. With a meat mallet, pound chicken to ¼˝ thickness; season with salt and black pepper. In a large skillet over medium-high heat, heat vegetable oil. Add chicken and cook about 3 minutes on each side. Remove chicken from skillet. Reduce heat, stir in broth mixture and return chicken to skillet. Cook 3 minutes more or until cooked through, turning to coat chicken with glaze.

Lemon Zested Chicken Breasts

Serves 4

Ingredients

¼ C. olive oil, plus
   more for brushing

3 T. minced garlic

⅓ C. dry white wine

1 T. lemon zest

2 T. lemon juice

1½ tsp. dried oregano

1 tsp. finely chopped
   fresh thyme

Salt and black pepper to taste

4 boneless, skin-on
   chicken breast halves

1 lemon

Directions

Preheat oven to 400°. In a small saucepan over medium-low heat, heat olive oil. Add garlic and cook for 1 minute, without allowing garlic to brown. Remove from heat and add wine, lemon zest, lemon juice, oregano and thyme. Pour mixture into a 9 x 13˝ baking pan.

Pat breast halves dry with paper towels and arrange over sauce in pan, skin side up. Brush chicken breasts with additional olive oil and season with salt and black pepper. Cut lemon into eight wedges and place in pan with chicken. Bake for 30 to 40 minutes or until cooked through and lightly browned. Broil for 2 minutes if more browning is desired. Remove from oven and cover pan tightly with aluminum foil for 10 minutes. Transfer chicken to individual serving plates and pour pan juices over the top of each.

Spicy Slow Cooker Chicken

Serves 6

Ingredients

- 6 bone-in, skinless chicken breast halves
- 1 T. chili powder
- Salt to taste
- ½ C. chicken broth
- 2 T. lemon juice
- ⅓ C. sliced pickled jalapeño peppers, drained
- 1 T. cornstarch
- 1 (8 oz.) pkg. Neufchâtel cheese, softened and cubed
- 2 bacon strips, cooked until crisp, crumbled

Directions

Coat a 6-quart slow cooker with nonstick cooking spray. Sprinkle breast halves with chili powder and salt; arrange in prepared slow cooker, bone side down. Add broth and lemon juice to cooker and top with jalapeño peppers. Cover and cook on low for 5 to 6 hours.

Transfer chicken and peppers to a serving platter; tent with aluminum foil. Turn slow cooker to high. In a small bowl, stir together cornstarch and 1 tablespoon water until smooth. Stir into cooking liquid. Add Neufchâtel cheese, stirring to combine. Cover and cook for 15 minutes or until cheese is melted and mixture is thickened. Pour sauce over chicken and sprinkle with bacon.

Crusty Parmesan Chicken

Serves 4

Ingredients

4 boneless, skinless chicken breast halves

½ C. mayonnaise

¼ C. grated Parmesan cheese

4 tsp. Italian seasoned dry bread crumbs

Directions

Preheat oven to 425°. Coat a 9 x 13″ baking pan with nonstick cooking spray and arrange breast halves in pan. In a small bowl, stir together mayonnaise and Parmesan cheese; divide mixture among breast halves and spread evenly. Sprinkle bread crumbs over the top. Bake for 20 minutes or until cooked through.

Chicken with Herbs

Serves 4

Ingredients

4 boneless, skinless
   chicken breast halves
2 T. olive oil
1 T. finely chopped onion
1 tsp. minced garlic
1 tsp. dried thyme
½ tsp. salt

½ tsp. black pepper
½ tsp. dried rosemary
¼ tsp. ground sage
Pinch of dried marjoram
Dash of hot sauce
1 T. chopped fresh parsley

Directions

Preheat oven to 425°. Coat a 7 x 11˝ baking pan with nonstick cooking spray and arrange breast halves in pan. In a small bowl, whisk together olive oil, onion, garlic, thyme, salt, black pepper, rosemary, sage, marjoram and hot sauce. Spread mixture evenly over chicken in pan. Bake for 30 to 40 minutes or until cooked through, basting with pan juices occasionally. Transfer breast halves to a serving platter, sprinkle with parsley and pour pan juices over the top.

Cheesy Mushroom Chicken

Ingredients

¼ C. butter
1 C. sliced fresh mushrooms
2 T. finely chopped shallot
Salt and black pepper to taste

4 boneless, skinless
  chicken breast halves
1 C. finely shredded
  mozzarella cheese

Directions

In a large skillet over medium heat, melt butter. Add mushrooms, shallot, salt and black pepper. Cook for 10 minutes or until mushrooms are tender and liquid is absorbed. Remove mushrooms and shallot from skillet and cover with aluminum foil to keep warm. Add breast halves to skillet and cook for 20 minutes or until cooked through, turning once during cooking time. Transfer chicken to a serving platter and sprinkle with mozzarella cheese. Pour mushroom mixture over the top. Let stand until cheese melts, covering with foil, if necessary.

Orange Chili
Slow Cooked Breasts

Serves 4

Ingredients

¾ C. enchilada sauce, any type

¼ C. barbecue sauce, any type

1 T. chili powder

1 tsp. ground cumin

4 bone-in, skinless chicken breast halves

3 T. orange marmalade

½ C. chopped fresh cilantro

2 tsp. orange zest

Directions

In a 6-quart slow cooker, stir together enchilada sauce and barbecue sauce. In a small bowl, stir together chili powder and cumin. Rub dry mixture over the surface of breast halves. Add breasts to slow cooker, turning to coat with sauce. Cover and cook on high for 3 to 4 hours or until chicken is cooked through.

Turn off cooker and transfer chicken to a serving platter. Add marmalade to sauce in cooker, stirring to blend. Stir in cilantro and orange zest and pour over chicken.

Note: *To heat things up a bit, add ¼ teaspoon or more crushed chipotle pepper to enchilada sauce mixture in slow cooker before adding chicken.*

Greek-Inspired Skillet

Serves 4

Ingredients

4 boneless, skinless
   chicken breast halves

Salt and black pepper to taste

1 T. olive oil

1½ C. sliced zucchini

¾ C. chopped green
   bell pepper

1 onion, sliced and
   separated into rings

1 tsp. minced garlic

1 (10.7 oz.) can tomato soup

2 C. hot cooked couscous*

½ C. crumbled feta cheese

Directions

Sprinkle breast halves with salt and black pepper. In a large skillet over medium heat, heat olive oil. Add chicken and cook for 12 to 15 minutes or until cooked through, turning once during cooking time. Remove chicken from pan and tent with aluminum foil; set aside.

To same skillet, add zucchini, bell pepper, onion, garlic and ¼ cup water. Reduce heat to low, cover and cook for 5 minutes, stirring occasionally. Stir in soup. Increase heat to medium and bring to a boil. Reduce heat to low, cover and simmer 5 minutes more, stirring occasionally.

Divide couscous evenly among individual serving plates and arrange chicken on top. Pour zucchini mixture over the top and sprinkle with feta cheese.

* To cook couscous, in a medium saucepan, bring 1 cup water and a pinch of salt to a boil. Stir in ⅔ cup quick-cooking couscous. Remove from heat, cover and let stand for 5 minutes. Fluff with a fork.

Spicy Peach-Glazed Chicken

Serves 8

Ingredients

1 jalapeño pepper, seeded

2 C. peach preserves

1 T. minced garlic

3 T. olive oil, plus more
for brushing

2 T. soy sauce

1 T. Dijon mustard

8 boneless, skin-on
chicken breast halves

Salt and black pepper to taste

4 ripe peaches, halved
and pitted

Directions

Finely chop jalapeño pepper and transfer to a medium bowl. Add preserves, garlic, 3 tablespoons olive oil, soy sauce and mustard; stir to combine. Set aside ½ cup of mixture.

Preheat grill to medium heat. Brush chicken breasts with olive oil and season with salt and black pepper. Place breasts on hot grill, skin side down, and cook for 11 to 13 minutes or until golden brown on both sides, turning halfway through cooking time. Brush both sides of chicken with peach mixture in bowl and cook 4 to 5 minutes longer. Discard any remaining peach mixture in bowl.

Place peach halves on grill, cut side down, and cook for 2 minutes. Turn over and brush with set-aside peach mixture. Grill 3 to 4 minutes longer or until peaches are soft. Serve grilled peach halves with chicken.

Roasted Garlic Chicken & Simple Risotto

Serves 4

Ingredients

1 T. butter

4 boneless, skinless chicken breast halves

1 (10.7 oz.) can cream of chicken soup

1 (10.7 oz.) can cream of mushroom with roasted garlic soup

2 C. uncooked instant white rice

1 C. frozen peas and carrots combination

Directions

In a large skillet over medium-high heat, melt butter. Add breast halves and cook for 10 minutes or until browned on both sides, turning halfway through cooking time. Remove chicken from skillet.

In same skillet, stir together cream of chicken and cream of mushroom soups; bring to a boil over medium heat. Stir in rice and vegetables. Arrange chicken on top, reduce heat to low, cover and cook for 5 minutes or until chicken is cooked through and rice is tender. Remove skillet from heat and let set for 5 minutes.

Buffalo-Style Grilled Chicken Breasts

Serves 4

Ingredients

½ C. butter

2 cloves garlic, chopped

2 T. plus 8 tsp. chili powder, or less to taste, divided

½ C. hot sauce

2 T. honey

Salt and black pepper to taste

8 tsp. ground cumin

Canola oil

4 boneless, skin-on chicken breast halves

½ C. heavy cream

½ C. sour cream

¼ C. chopped fresh parsley

1 C. crumbled blue cheese

Directions

In a medium saucepan over medium heat, melt butter. Add garlic and cook about 1 minute. Whisk in 2 tablespoons chili powder until well mixed. Stir in hot sauce, honey, salt and black pepper. Set aside ¼ cup; keep both portions warm.

Preheat grill to medium heat. Sprinkle 1 teaspoon chili powder, 1 teaspoon cumin and additional salt and black pepper on each side of each breast half. Drizzle both sides with canola oil. Grill uncovered, skin side down, until blackened. Turn chicken over, brush with some of the hot sauce mixture from saucepan and move to indirect heat. Cover and grill for 5 minutes or until cooked through, brushing occasionally with more sauce. Transfer chicken to a serving platter.

In a medium bowl, whisk together cream and sour cream. Stir in parsley, blue cheese and additional salt and black pepper. Pour cream mixture over chicken, and drizzle set-aside hot sauce mixture over the top.

Saucy Chicken Creole

Ingredients

1 (10.7 oz.) can cream
of chicken soup

1 (4.5 oz.) can chopped
green chiles, drained

1 tsp. lime juice

4 boneless, skinless
chicken breast halves

2 tsp. Creole or
Cajun seasoning

1 T. olive oil

¼ C. sour cream

Directions

In a medium bowl, stir together soup, chiles, lime juice and
½ cup water; set aside. Sprinkle chicken with Creole seasoning.
Heat olive oil in a large skillet over medium-high heat. Add
chicken and cook until dark golden brown on both sides. Add
set-aside soup mixture and bring to a boil. Reduce heat to low
and cook 5 minutes longer or until chicken is cooked through.
Stir in sour cream and cook until hot and bubbly. Transfer
chicken to a serving platter and pour sauce over the top.

Grilled Chicken Ratatouille

Serves 6

Ingredients

- 1 red onion
- 2 zucchini, halved lengthwise
- 1 Japanese eggplant, halved lengthwise
- 1 red bell pepper, quartered
- 2 tomatoes, halved crosswise
- 2 T. olive oil
- Salt and black pepper to taste
- 6 boneless, skinless chicken breast halves
- ⅓ C. chopped fresh basil
- 1½ tsp. red wine vinegar

Directions

Preheat grill to medium-high heat. Cut onion into ½″ wedges without cutting all the way through to root end. In a large bowl, combine onion, zucchini, eggplant, bell pepper and tomatoes. Drizzle olive oil over the top and season with salt and black pepper; toss gently to coat. Transfer vegetables to grill and cook until tender and slightly charred. Place chicken breasts in same bowl, turning to coat with remaining oil; season with salt and black pepper. Grill chicken for 12 minutes or until cooked through, turning once halfway through grilling time. Remove from heat and let set for 5 minutes.

Coarsely chop vegetables and transfer to a clean bowl. Stir in basil and vinegar; toss to coat. Season with salt and black pepper. Serve vegetables with chicken.

Chicken Breasts with Chive Sauce

Serves 4

Ingredients

4 boneless, skinless chicken breast halves

1 tsp. salt, divided

¼ C. plus 1 T. flour, divided

1 T. olive oil, divided

2 shallots, finely chopped

½ C. dry white wine

1 (14 oz.) can chicken broth

⅓ C. sour cream

1 T. Dijon mustard

½ C. chopped fresh chives

Directions

With a meat mallet, pound chicken to ½˝ thickness. Season with ½ teaspoon salt. Place ¼ cup flour in a pie plate. Heat 2 teaspoons olive oil in a large skillet over medium-high heat. Press both sides of breast halves into flour and add to skillet. Cook for 2 to 4 minutes or until golden brown, turning halfway through cooking time. Transfer chicken to a plate, cover and set aside.

Add remaining 1 teaspoon oil to same skillet and heat over medium-high heat. Add shallots, cooking for 1 to 2 minutes or until golden brown, scraping up any browned bits from bottom of skillet. Sprinkle with remaining 1 tablespoon flour and stir to coat. Add wine, broth and remaining ½ teaspoon salt; bring to a boil, stirring often. Return chicken and accumulated juices to pan; reduce heat to low and simmer for 5 to 10 minutes or until chicken is cooked through. Remove from heat and stir in sour cream, mustard and chives, turning chicken to coat.

Double-Dipped BBQ Chick

Serves 6

Ingredients

4 eggs

2 T. half & half

4 C. barbecue-flavored corn chips, finely crushed

¼ C. buttermilk powder

Purchased barbecue seasoning mix to taste*

3 boneless, skinless chicken breasts

Directions

Preheat oven to 425°. Line a rimmed baking sheet with parchment paper and set a wire rack on top; set aside. In a medium bowl, beat together eggs and half & half until fully combined. Place corn chips, buttermilk powder and seasoning mix in a large zippered plastic bag; close bag and shake to combine. Dip both sides of one chicken breast into egg mixture until coated, then shake in bag with corn chip mixture. Dip again in egg mixture and shake again in bag. Place breast on prepared baking sheet. Repeat with remaining breasts. Bake for 1 hour or until cooked through, covering with aluminum foil to prevent overbrowning, if necessary.

* Or use Big Batch Pantry Rub recipe, page 10 or Chili-Spice Blend, page 11.

UNDER THE KNIFE

When you chop and shred cooked chicken, you might want to prepare extra. Just pop the remainder in the freezer to use with future meals.

Breast Enhancement Tip #4

"Nipping and tucking" takes a steady hand and a sharp knife. If you have neither, step away from the breasts! In this chapter, you'll find all sorts of ways to use chopped, shredded and ground chicken.

Fiesta Chicken

Serves 2

Ingredients

⅓ C. biscuit baking mix
2 T. fat-free egg substitute
¼ C. plus 2 T. shredded
   Cheddar cheese

1 T. olive oil
1 boneless, skinless chicken
   breast, cut into ½˝ pieces
½ C. thick salsa, any variety

Directions

Preheat oven to 400°. Spray a 4 x 8˝ loaf pan with nonstick cooking spray. In a small bowl, stir together baking mix, egg substitute and 1 tablespoon water; spread evenly in prepared loaf pan. Sprinkle with ¼ cup Cheddar cheese.

In a large skillet over medium-high heat, heat olive oil. Add chicken and cook until the outside of chicken is no longer pink; drain and return chicken to skillet. Stir in salsa and cook until heated through. Pour mixture into loaf pan, spreading to within ½˝ of edges. Bake for 20 minutes; then sprinkle with remaining 2 tablespoons Cheddar cheese. Bake 2 minutes longer or until cheese is melted. Run a knife around edges of pan to loosen.

Slow-Cooked Shrimpy Chicken Jambalaya

Serves 8

Ingredients

- 1 lb. boneless, skinless chicken breasts, cut into ¾" pieces
- 2 C. thinly sliced celery
- 2 C. chopped onions
- 1 (14.5 oz.) can diced tomatoes, undrained
- 1 (14 oz.) can chicken broth
- ½ (6 oz.) can tomato paste
- 1½ tsp. Cajun seasoning
- 1 tsp. minced garlic
- 1½ C. uncooked instant brown rice
- ¾ C. chopped green, red and/or yellow sweet bell pepper
- 8 oz. fresh or frozen cooked shrimp, peeled and deveined, thawed
- 2 T. chopped fresh parsley

Directions

In a 4-quart slow cooker, combine chicken, celery, onions, tomatoes with juice, broth, tomato paste, Cajun seasoning and garlic. Cover and cook on low for 2½ hours.

Turn slow cooker to high, stir in rice and bell pepper. Cover and cook 30 minutes more or until most of the liquid is absorbed and rice is tender. Stir in shrimp and parsley.

Roasted Veggies with Chicken-Garden Wraps

Serves 4

Ingredients

2 C. shredded cooked chicken breast

½ C. shredded carrots

1 avocado, halved, pitted, peeled and thinly sliced

1 C. fresh baby spinach leaves

4 (8″) whole wheat flour tortillas

¼ C. low-fat dressing, any variety

Directions

Divide chicken, carrots, avocado and spinach evenly among tortillas. Drizzle dressing over the top. Roll each tortilla tightly; seal closed using toothpicks.

Popcorn Chicken

Serves 4

Ingredients

1 lb. boneless, skinless
  chicken breasts, cut
  into bite-size pieces

1 T. honey

2 tsp. seasoned salt, divided

1 egg

½ C. milk

1 C. flour

Canola oil

Directions

In a large bowl, stir together chicken, honey and ½ teaspoon seasoned salt. In a small bowl, beat together egg and milk. In a large zippered plastic bag, combine flour and remaining 1½ teaspoons seasoned salt; close bag and shake to mix. Dip chicken pieces in egg mixture; then shake in bag with flour mixture until chicken is well coated.

In a large saucepan, heat ½″ canola oil to 375°. Line a large plate with paper towels; set aside. Shake excess flour from chicken pieces and carefully place chicken in hot oil. Fry for 3 minutes or until golden brown. Remove from oil with a slotted spoon and transfer to prepared plate.

Buffalo'd Chicken Bites

Serves 4

Ingredients

1 egg white

⅓ C. buffalo wing sauce,
  any type

1 lb. boneless, skinless chicken
  breasts, cut into 1″ cubes

¾ C. biscuit baking mix

3 T. cornmeal

Salt and black pepper to taste

Vegetable oil

Directions

In a medium bowl, stir together egg white and wing sauce. Stir in chicken, cover and chill for 30 minutes.

Line a rimmed baking sheet with aluminum foil. Line another rimmed baking sheet with several layers of paper towels; set aside. In a large zippered plastic bag, combine baking mix, cornmeal, salt and black pepper. Close bag and shake to mix. Transfer about ¼ of the chicken pieces to bag using a slotted spoon. Close bag and shake to coat chicken. Transfer chicken to foil-lined baking sheet and repeat with remaining chicken and baking mixture.

In a large skillet over medium-high heat, heat about ½″ vegetable oil. Cook chicken in batches for 3 to 4 minutes or until golden brown on both sides, turning once. Transfer chicken to paper towel-lined baking sheet.

Note: *Make blue cheese dipping sauce by stirring together 3 ounces crumbled blue cheese, ⅓ cup sour cream, ⅓ cup mayonnaise and 2 to 3 tablespoons milk; chill. Serve with chicken bites.*

Buffalo Chicken Grilled Cheese

Serves 2

Ingredients

1 T. plain Greek yogurt

1 T. mayonnaise

Pinch of sugar

Garlic powder to taste

Salt and black pepper to taste

2 T. butter, softened, divided

¼ C. hot sauce

½ tsp. brown sugar

1 tsp. apple cider vinegar

¾ C. shredded cooked chicken breast

2 T. finely chopped onion

2 T. finely chopped celery

4 (½˝ thick) slices Italian bread

4 slices sharp Cheddar cheese

Directions

In a small bowl, stir together yogurt, mayonnaise, sugar, garlic powder, salt and black pepper; set aside. In a medium saucepan over medium-low heat, melt 1 tablespoon butter. Stir in hot sauce, brown sugar, vinegar, chicken, onion and celery until well blended; cook until heated through.

Spread about 1½ teaspoons butter over one side of each bread slice; place two bread slices on a sheet of waxed paper, butter side down. Spread about 1½ teaspoons set-aside yogurt mixture evenly over each bread slice; add one cheese slice to each. Top each with half the chicken mixture and one of the remaining cheese slices. Spread remaining yogurt mixture evenly over cheese and top each with one of the remaining bread slices, butter side up.

Preheat a large skillet over medium heat. When hot, place sandwiches in pan and cook until bottom is golden brown. Carefully flip sandwiches over and cook until the other side is golden brown.

Chicken Caesar Sliders

Serves 6

Ingredients

- ½ to ¾ C. Caesar salad dressing
- ½ C. grated Parmesan cheese, plus extra for serving
- ¼ C. chopped fresh parsley
- ½ tsp. black pepper
- 2 lbs. boneless, skinless chicken breasts, cooked and shredded
- 12 slider buns, split
- 2 C. shredded lettuce, optional

Directions

In a medium saucepan, stir together salad dressing, Parmesan cheese, parsley and black pepper; stir in chicken. Cover and cook over low heat until mixture is hot. Serve on buns with lettuce and extra Parmesan cheese, if desired.

Pulled Chicken Sandwiches

Serves 6

Ingredients

1 T. olive oil

¼ C. finely chopped onion

1 (8 oz.) can tomato sauce

2 T. tomato paste

1 T. Dijon mustard

1 T. Worcestershire sauce

1 tsp. honey

Salt and black pepper to taste

2 C. shredded cooked chicken breast

6 hamburger buns, split

Directions

In a medium saucepan over medium heat, heat olive oil. Add onion; cook for 3 minutes or until tender, stirring occasionally. Add tomato sauce, tomato paste, mustard, Worcestershire sauce and honey. Bring to a boil. Reduce heat and simmer for 5 minutes or until desired consistency. Season with salt and black pepper. Stir in chicken; heat through, stirring frequently. Serve on buns.

Lemon-Basil Chicken Salad

Serves 8

Ingredients

4 C. diced cooked chicken breast

1 celery rib, finely chopped

¼ C. chopped fresh basil

¼ C. slivered almonds

½ C. sour cream

½ C. mayonnaise

1½ tsp. lemon juice

Salt and black pepper to taste

Lettuce or buns, optional

Directions

In a medium bowl, stir together chicken, celery, basil and almonds. In a small bowl, stir together sour cream, mayonnaise, lemon juice, salt and black pepper. Add sour cream mixture to chicken mixture and toss to coat. Cover and chill. Serve on a bed of lettuce or on buns, if desired.

Waldorf Chicken Salad

Serves 6

Ingredients

½ C. chopped walnuts, toasted*

3 C. diced cooked chicken breast

1 C. seedless red grapes, halved

1 large Gala or Golden Delicious apple, diced

1 C. diced celery

½ C. mayonnaise

½ C. honey mustard

Salt and black pepper to taste

Lettuce or buns, optional

Directions

In a large bowl, stir together walnuts, chicken, grapes, apple, celery, mayonnaise and mustard. Season with salt and black pepper. Cover and chill. Serve on a bed of lettuce or on buns, if desired.

To toast, place walnuts in a single layer in a dry skillet over medium heat or in a baking pan in a 350° oven for approximately 10 minutes or until golden brown.

Mini Thai Chickie Pies

Serves 6

Ingredients

2 T. canola oil

1 lb. boneless, skinless
chicken breasts, cut
into bite-size pieces

½ C. chopped onion

4 green onions, sliced

¼ C. chopped fresh cilantro

½ tsp. red curry paste

1 T. lime juice

1 C. shredded
mozzarella cheese

½ C. biscuit baking mix

½ C. milk

2 eggs

⅓ C. salted peanuts
or cocktail peanuts

Directions

Preheat oven to 375°. Coat 12 muffin cups with nonstick cooking spray; set aside. In a large skillet over medium-high heat, heat canola oil. Add chicken and cook for 5 to 7 minutes or until cooked through, stirring occasionally. Add onion and cook about 3 minutes. Add green onions, cilantro, curry paste and lime juice, cooking until heated through, stirring occasionally. Cool about 5 minutes; then stir in mozzarella cheese.

In a medium bowl, stir together baking mix, milk and eggs until well blended; place 1 tablespoon mixture into each muffin cup. Add ¼ cup chicken mixture to each cup and top with 1 tablespoon remaining egg mixture. Bake for 10 minutes and sprinkle each with an equal amount of peanuts. Bake 20 to 25 minutes longer or until golden brown and a toothpick inserted in center comes out clean.

Remove from oven and let set for 5 minutes. Run a knife around the edge of each and remove pies to a cooling rack. Let cool for 10 minutes.

Individual Pot Pies

Serves 6

Ingredients

1 puff pastry sheet
from a 17.3 oz. pkg.

1 leek, sliced

½ C. butter, divided

2 C. sliced carrots

2 C. chopped asparagus

1 C. frozen peas, thawed

2 C. shredded cooked
chicken breast

½ C. flour

2 C. chicken stock

Salt and black pepper to taste

1 egg, beaten

Directions

Let pastry sheet set at room temperature for 30 minutes. Preheat oven to 375°. Coat six 10-ounce ramekins with nonstick cooking spray. Rinse leek in a bowl of cold water; drain. Set aside.

In a large saucepan over medium-high heat, melt 2 tablespoons butter. Add leek and carrots; cook for 5 minutes or until carrots begin to soften. Add asparagus and cook 5 minutes more or until vegetables are crisp-tender, stirring constantly. Remove from heat; stir in peas and chicken; set aside.

In a large saucepan over medium heat, melt remaining 6 tablespoons butter. Add flour, whisking until lightly browned. Gradually whisk in chicken stock; cook for 5 minutes or until sauce thickens. Season with salt and black pepper. Add sauce to chicken mixture; toss to combine. Set one prepared ramekin upside down on pastry and cut around it to create six pastry rounds.

Divide chicken mixture evenly among prepared ramekins. Place one pastry round over chicken mixture in each ramekin. Cut four slits in each. Brush beaten egg over the top of each pastry round. Set ramekins on a rimmed baking sheet and bake for 20 to 30 minutes or until crust is golden brown. Let cool for 5 minutes.

Mini Chicken Broccoli Pies

Serves 6

Ingredients

- 1 T. vegetable oil
- 1 lb. boneless, skinless chicken breasts, cut into bite-size pieces
- ½ C. chopped onion
- 1 C. frozen chopped broccoli, thawed and drained

- Salt and black pepper to taste
- 1 C. shredded Cheddar cheese
- ½ C. biscuit baking mix
- ½ C. milk
- 2 eggs

Directions

Preheat oven to 375°. Coat 12 muffin cups with nonstick cooking spray; set aside. In a large skillet over medium-high heat, heat vegetable oil. Add chicken and cook for 5 to 7 minutes or until cooked through, stirring occasionally. Add onion and cook for 2 minutes. Add broccoli, salt and black pepper, cooking until mixture is heated through, stirring occasionally. Cool for 5 minutes; then stir in Cheddar cheese.

In a medium bowl, stir together baking mix, milk and eggs, whisking until blended. Place 1 tablespoon egg mixture in each prepared muffin cup. Top with about ¼ cup chicken mixture; then cover with 1 tablespoon remaining egg mixture. Bake for 30 minutes or until a toothpick inserted in center comes out clean. Cool for 5 minutes; run a knife around the edge of each and remove pies to a cooling rack to cool for 10 minutes longer.

Mexican Chicken Soup

Serves 8

Ingredients

2 T. olive oil

¾ C. chopped onion

1½ tsp. minced garlic

1 red bell pepper, chopped

1 jalapeño pepper, seeded and finely chopped

1 T. smoked paprika

1 to 2 tsp. red pepper flakes

Salt and black pepper to taste

3 C. shredded cooked chicken breast

2 C. frozen corn kernels

4 C. chicken broth

2 tomatoes, chopped

1 (15 oz.) can black beans, drained and rinsed

¼ C. chopped fresh cilantro

½ C. crumbled feta cheese

Directions

In a large saucepan over medium-high heat, heat olive oil. Add onion, garlic, bell pepper and jalapeño pepper. Cook for 3 minutes; then add paprika, pepper flakes, salt and black pepper. Cook and stir briefly. Add chicken, corn, broth, tomatoes and beans. Bring to a boil; cover, reduce heat and simmer for 15 minutes. Transfer to individual serving bowls and garnish with cilantro and feta cheese.

Chicken Fiesta
à la Slow Cooker

Serves 8

Ingredients

½ C. chopped onion

1 green bell pepper, chopped

1 (16 oz.) jar salsa, any variety

3 C. chicken stock

1 (1.25 oz.) pkg. taco seasoning mix

1 (12 oz.) bag frozen corn

1 (6 oz.) can tomato paste

2 lbs. boneless, skinless chicken breasts

½ (8 oz.) pkg. cream cheese, cubed

½ C. sour cream

Shredded Mexican cheese blend

Tortilla strips

Directions

In a large slow cooker, combine onion, bell pepper, salsa, chicken stock, seasoning mix, corn, tomato paste and chicken. Cover and cook on low for 6 to 8 hours.

Remove chicken 30 minutes before serving time. Cube or shred chicken and return to slow cooker along with cream cheese and sour cream. Cook until cream cheese melts; stir. Transfer to individual serving bowls and garnish with Mexican cheese blend and tortilla strips.

Chicken & Barley Soup Pot

Serves 6

Ingredients

8 C. chicken stock
3 vegetable bouillon cubes
1½ tsp. dried thyme
1 tsp. poultry seasoning
1 T. dried parsley
½ C. finely chopped onion

1 C. chopped celery
1 C. diced carrots
½ C. pearl barley
2 C. diced cooked
  chicken breast
Salt and black pepper to taste

Directions

In a large saucepan over medium-high heat, combine chicken stock, bouillon cubes, thyme, poultry seasoning, parsley and 4 cups water. Bring to a boil; then reduce heat to low and simmer for 15 minutes.

Add onion, celery, carrots and barley to stock mixture in saucepan. Cook for 45 minutes; then stir in chicken, adding extra water if needed. Continue cooking until barley is tender. Season with salt and black pepper.

Roasted Potato, Kale & Chicken Stew

Serves 8

Ingredients

- 5 red potatoes, quartered
- 6 T. olive oil, divided
- Salt and black pepper to taste
- 5 mild sausage links, casings removed, sliced ½˝ thick
- 1 onion, chopped
- 1 shallot, chopped
- 3 carrots, chopped
- 6 C. chicken broth
- 1 tsp. dried thyme
- 1 chicken breast, cooked and shredded
- ¼ C. Parmesan cheese
- 5 C. chopped fresh kale
- 1 (15 oz.) can cannellini beans, drained and rinsed
- 1 to 2 T. flour

Directions

Preheat oven to 350°. Cover a rimmed baking sheet with aluminum foil. In a large bowl, combine potatoes, 3 tablespoons olive oil, salt and black pepper. Stir to coat potatoes. Transfer mixture to prepared baking sheet. Bake for 30 to 40 minutes or until potatoes are browned and tender; set aside.

Heat remaining 3 tablespoons olive oil in a large saucepan over medium heat. Add sausages, onion and shallot, stirring occasionally until sausage is cooked through. Add carrots, cooking until softened. Stir in broth, thyme, chicken, potatoes, Parmesan cheese, salt and black pepper. Bring to a simmer and add kale and beans. Simmer for 20 minutes or until kale is tender. In a small bowl, stir together flour and ½ cup cold water until smooth; stir into stew until thickened.

Sweet & Sour Chicken

Serves 4

Ingredients

1 C. cornstarch

2 eggs

¼ C. canola oil

4 boneless, skinless chicken breast halves, cubed

Salt and black pepper to taste

¾ C. sugar

¼ C. ketchup

½ C. distilled white vinegar

1 T. soy sauce

1 tsp. garlic salt

Directions

Preheat oven to 325°. Coat a 9 x 13˝ baking pan with nonstick cooking spray; set aside. Place cornstarch in a medium bowl. In a separate medium bowl, beat eggs. In a large skillet over medium heat, heat canola oil. Season chicken with salt and black pepper. Dredge chicken in cornstarch to coat thoroughly and then roll in egg. Carefully place chicken in hot oil and cook until just browned. Remove with a slotted spoon and transfer to prepared baking pan.

In a medium bowl, whisk together sugar, ketchup, vinegar, soy sauce and garlic salt until well combined; pour mixture over chicken in pan. Bake for 1 hour, turning chicken every 15 minutes.

Chicken Taquitos

Serves 10

Ingredients

6 oz. cream cheese, softened

½ C. green salsa, plus extra for serving

2 T. lime juice

¼ tsp. onion powder

1 tsp. chili powder

½ tsp. garlic powder

½ tsp. ground cumin

¼ C. chopped fresh cilantro

2 green onions, chopped

1½ C. shredded Monterey Jack cheese

2½ C. shredded cooked chicken breast

20 (6″) corn tortillas

Directions

Preheat oven to 400°. Line a rimmed baking sheet with aluminum foil and coat with nonstick cooking spray. In a large bowl, stir together cream cheese, salsa, lime juice, onion powder, chili powder, garlic powder and cumin until well blended. Fold in cilantro, green onions, Monterey Jack cheese and chicken.

Stack tortillas on a microwave-safe plate with a damp paper towel between each. Heat in microwave for 30 seconds or until softened. Spread about 3 tablespoons cream cheese mixture over one side of one tortilla. Roll up and place seam side down on prepared baking sheet. Continue with remaining tortillas and cream cheese mixture, spacing them evenly apart on baking sheet. Spray tortillas with nonstick cooking spray and bake for 15 to 20 minutes or until edges are golden brown. Serve with extra salsa.

Chicken Empanadas

Serves 6

Ingredients

- 3 C. chopped cooked chicken breast
- 1½ tsp. salt
- ½ tsp. black pepper
- 1 T. ground cumin
- 1 jalapeño pepper, seeded and chopped
- ¼ C. chopped red bell pepper
- ½ (8 oz.) pkg. cream cheese, softened
- 2 C. shredded Colby Jack cheese
- 1 (15 oz.) pkg. refrigerated pie crusts, softened according to package directions

Directions

Preheat oven to 400°. Coat a rimmed baking sheet with nonstick cooking spray; set aside. In a large bowl, stir together chicken, salt, black pepper, cumin, jalapeño pepper, bell pepper, cream cheese and Colby Jack cheese; set aside.

On a lightly floured surface, unroll pie crust. Using a 3˝ cookie cutter, cut six rounds, rerolling scraps. Repeat with remaining pie crust. Lightly brush edges of one round with water. Place 1 heaping teaspoon chicken mixture in center and fold dough in half over filling, pressing edges of dough with a fork to seal. Transfer to prepared baking sheet. Repeat with remaining rounds and chicken mixture. Bake for 15 minutes.

South American Chicken Tacos

Serves 4

Ingredients

1 T. vegetable oil

1 lb. ground chicken breast

½ C. finely chopped onion

2 tsp. ground coriander

2 tsp. ground cumin

1 (14.5 oz.) can diced tomatoes, undrained

1 potato, peeled and finely chopped

¼ C. chopped pitted dried plums

¼ C. chopped green olives with pimiento

12 (6˝) corn or flour tortillas

1 C. shredded Monterey Jack cheese

Fresh cilantro

Directions

Preheat oven to 350°. Heat vegetable oil in a large skillet over medium heat. Add chicken and onion, cooking until chicken is no longer pink, stirring occasionally to crumble; drain. Stir in coriander and cumin. Cook for 2 minutes. Add tomatoes with juice, potato, plums and olives. Bring to a boil. Reduce heat, cover and simmer for 12 to 15 minutes or until potato is tender. Uncover and cook 5 minutes more or until most of the liquid has evaporated. Meanwhile, wrap tortillas in aluminum foil and bake for 15 minutes.

Place about ⅓ cup chicken mixture in the center of each tortilla. Top with Monterey Jack cheese and cilantro. Fold tortillas in half to serve.

Quick-Chick Pasta Primavera

Serves 4

Ingredients

- ½ (16 oz.) pkg. uncooked whole wheat rotini pasta
- 2 T. vegetable oil
- 1 lb. boneless, skinless chicken breasts, cut into bite-size pieces
- 1 lb. frozen broccoli, carrots and pepper blend, thawed
- ½ (8 oz.) pkg Neufchâtel cheese, softened
- ½ C. Italian salad dressing
- ½ C. milk

Directions

In a large saucepan of boiling water, cook rotini according to package directions; drain. Meanwhile, in a large skillet over medium-high heat, heat vegetable oil. Add chicken and cook until no longer pink; drain. Stir in vegetables and pasta.

In a small bowl, whisk together Neufchâtel cheese, salad dressing and milk until smooth. Stir into chicken mixture. Cook over medium heat until heated through.

Chicken à la King

Serves 4

Ingredients

- 1 (8 ct.) pkg. refrigerated buttermilk biscuits
- 1½ lbs. boneless, skinless chicken breasts, cut into bite-size pieces
- ½ C. flour
- 2 T. canola oil, divided
- 10 oz. fresh white mushrooms, quartered
- 1 green bell pepper, diced
- ½ tsp. salt
- ½ tsp. black pepper
- 1 C. dry sherry
- 1 C. chicken broth
- 1 C. milk
- 1 (4 oz.) jar diced pimento, drained
- ½ C. sliced green onions

Directions

Bake biscuits according to package directions. Meanwhile, in a medium bowl, toss chicken in flour until coated. In a large skillet over medium-high heat, heat 1 tablespoon canola oil. Add chicken and cook for 3 to 4 minutes or until lightly browned. Transfer chicken to a plate. Set aside flour remaining in bowl. Reduce heat to medium. Add remaining 1 tablespoon oil to skillet. Add mushrooms, bell pepper, salt and black pepper and cook for 3 to 4 minutes or until mushrooms are soft and starting to brown, stirring frequently. Add sherry; bring to a boil and cook for 3 minutes, scraping up any browned bits from the bottom of skillet.

To bowl of set-aside flour, add broth and milk, whisking until smooth. Add to skillet with mushroom mixture and bring to a simmer, stirring frequently. Add pimento and chicken and return to a simmer, stirring constantly. Reduce heat and simmer for 5 to 6 minutes or until vegetables are tender and chicken is cooked through. Stir in green onions just before serving over biscuits.

Sweet & Savory Cranberry Fillets

Serves 4

Ingredients

1 C. dried sweetened cranberries

½ C. apple juice

½ C. chicken stock

¼ C. flour

½ tsp. salt

½ tsp. coarsely ground black pepper

4 boneless, skinless chicken breast fillets

1 T. vegetable oil

1 T. Dijon mustard

Directions

In a small bowl, stir together cranberries, apple juice and chicken stock; set aside.

In a large zippered plastic bag, combine flour, salt and black pepper. Close bag and shake to mix. Add chicken fillets. Turn to coat chicken. In a medium skillet over medium-high heat, heat vegetable oil. Add chicken and cook for 10 minutes, turning once halfway through cooking time. Transfer chicken to a plate.

Transfer set-aside cranberry mixture to hot skillet and cook over low heat, scraping up browned bits from bottom of skillet. Stir in mustard. Add chicken and cook 8 to 10 minutes more or until chicken is cooked through and sauce has thickened. Transfer chicken to a serving platter and pour sauce over chicken.

Zinger Chicken Kabobs

Serves 4

Ingredients

½ to 1 T. minced garlic

1½ tsp. smoked paprika

½ tsp. cayenne pepper

2 tsp. dried thyme

2 T. olive oil

2 tsp. salt

2 lbs. boneless, skin-on chicken breasts, cut into bite-size pieces

½ onion, cut into 1˝ pieces

1 red bell pepper, cut into 1˝ pieces

Chopped fresh chives, optional

Directions

In a large bowl, stir together garlic, paprika, cayenne pepper, thyme, olive oil and salt. Add chicken, turning to coat evenly. Cover and refrigerate for at least 3 hours. If using wooden skewers, soak them in cold water for 1 hour before adding food to prevent burning.

Drain liquid from chicken. Thread as many chicken, onion and bell pepper pieces as possible onto each skewer, leaving about ½˝ between pieces. Preheat grill to medium-high heat. Grill kabobs for 9 minutes or until cooked through, turning halfway through grilling time. Remove food from skewers and transfer to a serving platter; garnish with chives, if desired.

Grilled Chicken Fajitas

Serves 6

Ingredients

¼ C. lime juice

¼ C. chicken broth

3 scallions, cut into 1″ pieces

1 tsp. minced garlic

1 T. honey

Salt to taste

1 C. packed fresh cilantro leaves

1½ lbs. boneless, skinless chicken breasts

1 onion, sliced ½″ thick

1 orange bell pepper, quartered

1 yellow bell pepper, quartered

1 avocado, halved, pitted and peeled

¼ C. plain Greek yogurt

2 tsp. olive oil

Dash of ground cumin

Dash of ground coriander

12 (6″) corn tortillas

Directions

Place lime juice, broth, scallions, garlic, honey, salt and cilantro in a blender container. Process until smooth; set aside ¼ cup of mixture. Place chicken breasts in a medium bowl. Place onion and bell peppers in a separate medium bowl. Divide cilantro mixture from blender evenly among the two bowls; toss to coat and let stand at room temperature for 20 minutes to marinate. Meanwhile, to blender, add avocado, set-aside cilantro mixture and ½ cup water. Process until smooth.

Place yogurt in a small bowl. In a small skillet over medium heat, heat olive oil. Add cumin and coriander, and cook for 1 minute, stirring constantly. Pour mixture over yogurt; set aside until serving time and then stir.

Preheat grill to medium-high heat. Grill chicken for 12 to 15 minutes or until cooked through. Remove from grill and cover with aluminum foil. Grill onion and bell peppers for 5 minutes or until tender. Heat tortillas on grill for 30 seconds. Slice chicken and vegetables into thin strips; divide evenly among tortillas. Top with set-aside cilantro, yogurt and avocado mixtures.

Chicken Lasagna Rolls

Serves 5

Ingredients

10 uncooked lasagna noodles

6 T. butter

1 onion, chopped

½ C. chopped red bell pepper

½ C. chopped almonds

½ C. cornstarch

Salt and black pepper to taste

2 (10.5 oz.) cans chicken broth

2 C. chopped cooked chicken breast

1 (10 oz.) pkg. frozen chopped spinach, thawed and drained*

2 C. milk

½ C. shredded Swiss cheese, divided

¼ C. shredded Parmesan cheese

¼ C. white grape juice

Directions

Preheat oven to 350°. In a large saucepan of boiling water, cook lasagna noodles according to package directions; drain, remove from saucepan and set aside. In the same saucepan over medium heat, melt butter. Add onion, bell pepper and almonds, stirring until almonds are lightly browned. Stir in cornstarch, salt and black pepper until well blended. Stir in broth; bring to a boil and cook until thickened, stirring constantly. Transfer half the mixture to a large bowl; stir in chicken and spinach.

Coat a 7 x 11˝ baking pan with nonstick cooking spray. Spread about 3 tablespoons chicken mixture along the length of each noodle. Roll up and place in prepared pan, seam side down.

To remaining mixture in saucepan, stir in milk, ¼ cup Swiss cheese, Parmesan cheese and grape juice. Cook over medium heat until thick, stirring constantly. Pour mixture over lasagna rolls. Bake for 25 minutes. Sprinkle with remaining ¼ cup Swiss cheese. Bake 5 minutes more or until cheese melts.

* Place thawed spinach on a clean kitchen towel. Above the sink, squeeze towel around spinach to remove all excess liquid.

Chicken & Dumpling Casserole

Serves 8

Ingredients

¼ C. butter

½ C. chopped onion

½ C. chopped celery

1 tsp. minced garlic

½ C. flour

2 tsp. sugar

1 tsp. salt

½ tsp. black pepper

1 T. dried basil, divided

4 C. chicken broth

1 (10 oz.) pkg. frozen green peas

4 C. cubed cooked chicken breast

2 C. biscuit baking mix

⅔ C. milk

Directions

Preheat oven to 350°. Coat a 9 x 13″ baking pan with nonstick cooking spray; set aside. In a large saucepan over medium heat, melt butter. Add onion and celery; cook until tender, stirring occasionally. Add garlic and cook 1 minute longer. Stir in flour, sugar, salt, black pepper and 1 teaspoon basil until well blended. Gradually stir in broth. Bring to a boil and cook for 1 minute or until thickened, stirring constantly. Reduce heat, add peas and cook for 5 minutes, stirring constantly. Stir in chicken. Transfer to prepared baking pan.

In a small bowl, combine baking mix and remaining 2 teaspoons basil. With a fork, stir in milk until moistened. Drop by tablespoonfuls into 12 mounds over chicken mixture. Bake for 30 minutes. Cover with aluminum foil and bake 10 minutes longer or until a toothpick inserted in a dumpling comes out clean.

Chicken Enchiladas

Serves 10

Ingredients

- 1 (8 oz.) pkg. cream cheese, softened
- 2 tsp. onion powder
- 2 tsp. ground cumin
- Salt and black pepper to taste
- 5 C. diced cooked chicken breast
- 20 (6″) flour tortillas at room temperature
- 2 (10.7 oz.) cans cream of chicken soup
- 1 (16 oz.) container sour cream
- 1 C. milk
- 2 (4 oz.) cans chopped green chiles, drained
- 2 C. shredded Cheddar cheese

Directions

Preheat oven to 350°. Coat two 9 x 13″ baking pans with nonstick cooking spray; set aside. In a large mixing bowl, beat together cream cheese, onion powder, cumin, salt, black pepper and 2 tablespoons water on medium speed until smooth and creamy. Stir in chicken. Spread ¼ cup chicken mixture along the center of each tortilla. Roll up and arrange in prepared baking pans, seam side down.

In a large bowl, stir together soup, sour cream, milk and chiles; pour over enchiladas. Bake for 30 to 40 minutes or until heated through. Sprinkle with Cheddar cheese and bake 5 minutes longer or until cheese is melted.

Individual Asian-Style Pizzas

Serves 4

Ingredients

4 (6″) whole wheat pita bread rounds

1 C. sliced fresh white mushrooms

⅔ C. thinly sliced fresh pea pods

½ C. coarsely shredded carrots

1½ C. chopped cooked chicken breast

¼ C. sliced green onions

¼ C. prepared peanut sauce*

2 T. chopped unsalted peanuts

Directions

Preheat oven to 450°. Place pita bread rounds on an ungreased baking sheet. Bake for 8 minutes or until lightly brown and crisp, turning once during baking time. Meanwhile, coat a large skillet with nonstick cooking spray and heat over medium heat. Add mushrooms, pea pods and carrots. Cook for 3 minutes or until just tender. Stir in chicken and green onions. Remove from heat.

Spread each pita bread round with 1 tablespoon peanut sauce. Top with chicken mixture and sprinkle with peanuts.

* Or use Peanut Sauce recipe, page 120.

Garlic-y Chicken & Noodles

Serves 4

Ingredients

½ (12 oz.) pkg. uncooked
 extra-wide egg noodles

½ slice white bread

¾ C. shredded Parmesan
 cheese, divided

2 T. butter, melted

2 to 2½ lbs. boneless,
 skinless chicken breasts,
 cooked and shredded

1 C. frozen peas

2 tsp. minced garlic

1¾ C. milk

Directions

Preheat oven to 450°. Coat four individual casserole dishes with nonstick cooking spray; set aside. In a large saucepan of boiling water, cook egg noodles according to package directions; drain. Meanwhile, in a food processor, process bread until coarse crumbs remain; transfer to a small bowl and stir in ¼ cup Parmesan cheese and butter. Set aside.

In a large saucepan over medium heat, stir together chicken, peas, garlic and milk until heated through. Stir in noodles and remaining ½ cup Parmesan cheese, cooking until bubbly. Divide mixture evenly among prepared casserole dishes. Top each with an equal amount of bread crumb mixture. Bake for 5 minutes or until lightly browned.

SHOW 'EM OFF

A simple chicken breast can be dressed up and enhanced in many different ways. In this chapter, each recipe is followed by a serving idea for your convenience.

Breast Enhancement Tip #5

If you feel your breasts are a little Plain-Jane and boring, perk them up a bit. Try these recipes that are great for adding a bit of flair to a simple breast!

Tomatoes & Cukes

Makes about 2 cups

Ingredients

1 tomato

½ cucumber

2 T. finely chopped onion

2 T. chopped fresh cilantro

1 T. lime juice

½ tsp. salt

Directions

Seed and chop tomato. Peel, seed and chop cucumber. Transfer to a small bowl. Add onion, cilantro, lime juice and salt; stir to combine. Refrigerate for 30 minutes.

Serving Idea: *Serve Tomatoes & Cukes over grilled chicken.*

Fruit Salsa

Makes about 4 1/2 cups

Ingredients

1½ C. cubed fresh pineapple

3 kiwifruit, peeled and cubed

¾ C. coarsely chopped fresh orange sections

½ C. peeled, chopped fresh mango

½ C. diced onion

2 T. chopped fresh cilantro

1½ tsp. ground cumin

¼ tsp. salt

Pinch of black pepper

1 jalapeño pepper, seeded and chopped

Directions

In a medium bowl, stir together pineapple, kiwifruit, orange, mango, onion, cilantro, cumin, salt, black pepper and jalapeño pepper.

Serving Idea: *Serve Fruit Salsa over broiled chicken.*

Mango-Tango Salsa

Makes about 2 cups

Ingredients

2 T. rice wine vinegar

2 T. olive oil

¼ tsp. ground cumin

Salt and black pepper to taste

1 avocado, halved, pitted, peeled and chopped

⅔ C. chopped fresh mango

⅓ C. chopped red bell pepper

¼ C. chopped fresh cilantro

2 jalapeño peppers, seeded and finely chopped

Directions

In a large bowl, whisk together vinegar, olive oil, cumin, salt and black pepper. Stir in avocado, mango, bell pepper, cilantro and jalapeño peppers. Serve promptly.

Serving Idea: *Serve Mango-Tango Salsa over Cajun-seasoned grilled chicken.*

Blueberry Chutney with Ginger

Makes about 1¹/2 cups

Ingredients

2 C. fresh or frozen blueberries, thawed

⅓ C. brown sugar

⅓ C. finely chopped onion

¼ C. golden raisins

3 T. apple cider vinegar

¼ tsp. ground ginger

¼ tsp. salt

¼ tsp. ground cinnamon

Pinch of red pepper flakes

Pinch of ground cloves

½ tsp. minced garlic

Directions

In a medium saucepan over medium heat, combine blueberries, brown sugar, onion, raisins, vinegar, ginger, salt, cinnamon, pepper flakes, cloves and garlic. Bring to a boil, stirring constantly. Reduce heat to medium-low and simmer for 25 minutes or until thickened, stirring occasionally.

Serving Idea: *Serve Blueberry Chutney with Ginger over Italian-seasoned baked chicken.*

Tangy Bacon Sauce

Makes about 3 cups

Ingredients

4 bacon strips
¼ C. finely chopped onion
1½ C. unsweetened
   apple cider

1 C. chicken broth
1 T. flour
1 T. chopped fresh parsley

Directions

In a large skillet over medium heat, cook bacon until crisp. Remove bacon from skillet, crumble and set aside. Add onion to skillet and cook for 2 minutes, stirring frequently. Stir in apple cider and broth; bring to a boil and boil for 2 minutes, stirring occasionally. Whisk in flour until smooth. Stir in set-aside bacon and parsley.

Serving Idea: *Serve Tangy Bacon Sauce over fried chicken breasts and hot cooked rice.*

Blackberry-Wine Sauce

Makes about 1 cup

Ingredients

1½ C. fresh blackberries

1 T. butter

½ C. finely chopped onion

½ C. dry red wine

1 T. lemon juice

¼ C. seedless blackberry jam

¼ tsp. salt

¼ tsp. coarsely ground
black pepper

Directions

Place blackberries in a food processor and puree until smooth. Push through a fine mesh strainer; set aside.

In a small skillet over medium-low heat, melt butter. Add onion and cook for 10 minutes or until tender, stirring occasionally. Add wine and lemon juice. Bring to a boil. Reduce heat to low and simmer until mixture is reduced by about half. In a small bowl, stir together set-aside blackberries, jam, salt and black pepper; add to wine mixture, stirring to combine. Increase heat to medium and bring to a boil. Reduce heat to low and simmer for 5 minutes, stirring frequently.

Serving Idea: *Serve Blackberry-Wine Sauce with grilled chicken kabobs.*

Mushroom & Sage Sauce

Makes about 2 cups

Ingredients

3 T. butter
½ C. chopped shallot
10 oz. fresh cremini
  mushrooms, thickly sliced
1 tsp. chopped fresh parsley

1 C. dry white wine
⅔ C. heavy cream
1½ tsp. dried sage
Salt and black pepper to taste

Directions

In a large skillet over medium-high heat, melt butter. Add shallot and cook for 1 minute. Add mushrooms and parsley and cook 5 to 10 minutes more or until mushrooms have browned. Add wine, scraping up browned bits from bottom of skillet. Stir in cream. Bring to a boil and cook for 10 minutes or until thick. Remove from heat, stir in sage and season with salt and black pepper.

Serving Idea: *Serve Mushroom & Sage Sauce over pan-fried chicken breast cutlets.*

Citrus Sauce

Makes about 2¼ cups

Ingredients

1 (8 oz.) can crushed
  pineapple, undrained

1 T. sugar

1 T. cornstarch

Salt and black pepper to taste

½ tsp. ground allspice

Pinch each of ground
  cinnamon, nutmeg
  and ginger

1 C. orange juice

1 T. butter

1 T. orange zest

1 T. lemon zest

Directions

Drain pineapple, reserving juice. Add enough water to juice, if needed, to measure ½ cup liquid; set aside. In a medium saucepan, stir together sugar, cornstarch, salt, black pepper, allspice, cinnamon, nutmeg and ginger. Slowly stir in pineapple, pineapple juice and orange juice until combined. Stir in butter, orange zest and lemon zest. Bring to a boil and cook over medium-high heat until mixture thickens.

Serving Idea: *Serve Citrus Sauce over baked chicken breasts and rice.*

Barbeque Sauce

Makes about 2 cups

Ingredients

1 (6 oz.) can tomato paste
¾ C. brown sugar
3 T. Dijon mustard
2 T. BBQ seasoning mix*

2 T. Worcestershire sauce
1 tsp. salt
½ tsp. black pepper

Directions

In a large saucepan over medium-high heat, whisk together tomato paste, brown sugar, mustard, seasoning mix, Worcestershire sauce, salt, black pepper and 4 cups water; bring to a boil. Reduce heat to low and simmer until thickened, stirring occasionally.

Serving Idea: *Transfer half the sauce to a separate bowl and set aside to serve with chicken. Brush remaining sauce on chicken while grilling.*

* Or use Big Batch Pantry Rub recipe, page 10 or Chili-Spice Blend, page 11.

Sweet Cranberry BBQ Sauce

Makes about 3¹/₂ cups

Ingredients

2 C. fresh or frozen
   cranberries, thawed

1½ C. honey

1½ C. ketchup

1 C. red wine vinegar

2 T. lemon juice

2 T. Worcestershire sauce

½ tsp. coarsely ground
   black pepper

Directions

In a medium saucepan over medium-high heat, stir together cranberries, honey, ketchup, vinegar, lemon juice, Worcestershire sauce and black pepper. Bring to a boil. Reduce heat, cover and simmer for 20 minutes. Uncover and simmer 20 minutes more or until thickened.

Serving Idea: *Serve Sweet Cranberry BBQ Sauce as a dipping sauce with chicken fingers. Or brush over chicken during baking.*

Apple Onion Sauce

Makes about 1³/4 cups

Ingredients

1 to 2 T. vegetable oil

1 onion, coarsely chopped

1 Gravenstein, Cortland or other cooking apple, cored and coarsely chopped

3 T. apple cider vinegar

1½ C. chicken broth

2 T. butter

Salt and black pepper to taste

Directions

In a large skillet over medium heat, heat vegetable oil. Add onion and apple. Increase heat to high and cook for 2 minutes or until apple is golden brown, stirring constantly. Add vinegar, scraping up browned bits from bottom of skillet, stirring constantly. Bring to a boil and cook for 1 minute or until mixture becomes syrupy. Stir in broth and return to a boil. Cook until mixture is reduced by about half. Remove from heat. Add butter, stirring until melted; season with salt and black pepper.

Serving Idea: *Serve Apple Onion Sauce with baked chicken.*

Rémoulade Sauce

Makes about 1 cup

Ingredients

¾ C. mayonnaise

4½ tsp. dill pickle relish

1 tsp. finely chopped capers

1 T. lemon juice

1 T. Dijon mustard

2 tsp. chopped fresh parsley

¼ tsp. dried tarragon

Hot sauce to taste

Directions

In a small bowl, stir together mayonnaise, relish, capers, lemon juice, mustard, parsley, tarragon and hot sauce. Cover and refrigerate until serving time.

Serving Idea: *Serve Rémoulade Sauce over chicken burgers or as a dipping sauce for Popcorn Chicken, page 75.*

Garlic & Red Wine Sauce

Makes about ³/4 cup

Ingredients

3 T. finely chopped shallot
3 T. minced garlic
Salt and black pepper to taste

1½ C. chicken stock
½ C. dry red wine
2 T. butter, softened

Directions

In a small saucepan over high heat, combine shallot, garlic, salt and black pepper. Stir in chicken stock and wine; bring to a boil and cook for 15 minutes. Add butter, remove from heat and stir until butter is melted.

Serving Idea: *Serve Garlic & Red Wine Sauce over roasted chicken.*

Creamy Horseradish Sauce

Makes about 1¼ cups

Ingredients

1 C. sour cream
¼ C. grated fresh horseradish
1 T. Dijon mustard

1 tsp. white wine vinegar
½ tsp. salt
½ tsp. black pepper

Directions

In a medium bowl, whisk together sour cream, horseradish, mustard, vinegar, salt and black pepper. Cover and refrigerate overnight.

Serving Idea: *Serve Creamy Horseradish Sauce as a dipping sauce with chicken kabobs.*

Tomato-Butter Sauce

Makes about 2 cups

Ingredients

¼ C. plus 2 T. finely chopped shallot

1 C. dry white wine

Salt and cayenne pepper to taste

¼ C. heavy cream

¾ C. butter, cubed

¼ tsp. hot sauce

½ tsp. Worcestershire sauce

2 T. finely chopped capers

¾ C. diced fresh tomatoes

Directions

In a medium saucepan over medium heat, combine ¼ cup shallot and wine. Season with salt and cayenne pepper and bring to a boil. Reduce heat to medium-low and simmer until mixture is reduced by about half. Add cream and cook for 2 minutes. Remove from heat and whisk in butter, a little at a time until melted. Whisk in hot sauce and Worcestershire sauce. Drain through a fine mesh strainer, discarding solids. Return liquid to saucepan and add remaining 2 tablespoons shallot, capers and tomatoes. Stir well and keep warm.

Serving Idea: *Serve Tomato-Butter Sauce over roasted chicken and vegetables.*

Quick Dipping Sauce

Makes about 1¹/₄ cups

Ingredients

1 C. ketchup

¼ C. honey

1 T. prepared yellow mustard

½ tsp. ground nutmeg

Directions

In a small bowl, whisk together ketchup, honey, mustard and nutmeg until well blended and smooth.

Serving Idea: *Serve Quick Dipping Sauce with chicken fingers or Popcorn Chicken, page 75.*

Peanut Sauce

Makes about 1 cup

Ingredients

2 T. coconut cream

1 T. plus 1 tsp. red curry paste

1 C. chicken broth

¼ C. unsweetened
   coconut milk

¼ C. crunchy peanut butter

1 T. fish sauce

1 T. lime juice

Directions

In a small saucepan over medium heat, cook coconut cream for 2 minutes or until hot. Stir in curry paste and cook 2 minutes more. Whisk in broth, coconut milk, peanut butter and fish sauce. Increase heat to medium-high and bring to a boil. Reduce heat and simmer for 10 minutes or until thickened, stirring constantly. Cool to room temperature. Whisk in lime juice just before serving.

Serving Idea: *Serve Peanut Sauce with chicken stir-fry.*

Marsala Sauce

Makes about 1 cup

Ingredients

1 T. plus ¼ C. butter, divided

1 (8 oz.) pkg. fresh white mushrooms, sliced

2 oz. prosciutto, thinly sliced

1 shallot, finely chopped

½ C. dry Marsala wine

¼ C. chicken stock

1 T. chopped fresh parsley

Salt and black pepper to taste

Directions

In a medium skillet over medium-high heat, melt 1 tablespoon butter. Add mushrooms, prosciutto and shallot; cook for 3 to 4 minutes or until shallot is translucent. Add wine and chicken stock. Increase heat to high and cook for 5 minutes or until liquid is reduced by half. Reduce heat to low; stir in parsley and remaining ¼ cup butter. When butter is melted, season with salt and black pepper.

Serving Idea: *Serve Marsala Sauce over pan-fried chicken breasts.*

Chimichurri

Makes about 1 cup

Ingredients

- 1 bunch parsley, finely chopped
- 1 bunch cilantro, finely chopped
- 3 T. capers, finely chopped
- 1 tsp. minced garlic

- 1½ T. red wine vinegar
- 1 tsp. salt
- ½ tsp. red pepper flakes
- ½ tsp. black pepper
- ½ C. olive oil

Directions

In a medium bowl, toss together parsley, cilantro, capers and garlic. Add vinegar, salt, pepper flakes and black pepper; stir to combine. Add olive oil and mix until well combined. Let set at room temperature for 30 minutes.

Serving Idea: *Serve Chimichurri with grilled chicken.*

Sour Cream Gravy

Makes about 2 cups

Ingredients

3 T. butter
1 shallot, finely chopped
½ tsp. minced garlic
¼ C. flour

1½ C. chicken broth
1 C. sour cream
Salt and black pepper to taste

Directions

In a medium saucepan over medium-low heat, melt butter. Add shallot and garlic and cook for 2 minutes or until tender, stirring constantly. Whisk in flour until well blended. Slowly whisk in broth until bubbly and thickened. Whisk in sour cream until mixture just begins to simmer. Remove from heat and season with salt and black pepper.

Serving Idea: *Serve Sour Cream Gravy over fried chicken and mashed potatoes.*

Parmesan-Basil Pesto

Makes about ½ cup

Ingredients

1½ C. packed fresh basil
½ tsp. salt
¼ tsp. black pepper
¼ C. grated Parmesan cheese

2 T. pine nuts, toasted*
1 tsp. minced garlic
½ C. olive oil

Directions

In a food processor, combine basil, salt and black pepper. Process until basil is chopped. Add Parmesan cheese, pine nuts and garlic. With food processor running, add olive oil in a thin stream until mixture is nearly smooth.

Serving Idea: *Serve Parmesan-Basil Pesto with baked chicken tenders and cooked pasta.*

* To toast, place pine nuts in a single layer in a dry skillet over medium heat or in a baking pan in a 350° oven for approximately 10 minutes or until golden brown.

INDEX

Soaks, Rubs & Body Butters

Implants

Size Matters

Under the Knife

Show 'Em Off